ICE Design and Construct

Conditions of Contract

CONDITIONS OF CONTRACT AND FORMS OF TENDER, AGREEMENT
AND BOND FOR USE IN CONNECTION WITH WORKS OF CIVIL
ENGINEERING CONSTRUCTION

Institution of Civil Engineers
Association of Consulting Engineers
Federation of Civil Engineering Contractors

Published for the Institution of Civil Engineers, the Association of Consulting Engineers and the Federation of Civil Engineering Contractors by Thomas Telford Services Ltd, Thomas Telford House, 1 Heron Quay, London E14 4JD

Copies may also be obtained from
  The Director General and Secretary
  The Institution of Civil Engineers
  1–7 Great George Street
  London SW1P 3AA

  The Secretary
  The Association of Consulting Engineers
  Alliance House
  12 Caxton Street
  London SW1H 0QL

  The General Secretary
  The Federation of Civil Engineering Contractors
  Cowdray House
  6 Portugal Street
  London WC2A 2HH

First edition published 1992, reprinted 1997

The Institution of Civil Engineers, the Association of Consulting Engineers and the Federation of Civil Engineering Contractors have, as sponsoring authorities, approved this first edition of the document to be known as the ICE Design and Construct Conditions of Contract for works of civil engineering construction. A permanent joint committee has prepared and will keep under review the use of the document and will consider any suggestions for amendment, which should be addressed to the Director General and Secretary (CCSJC), the Institution of Civil Engineers, 1–7 Great George Street, London SW1P 3AA. Revision to the document will be made when such action seems warranted.

A CIP cataloguing record for this book is available from the British Library

ISBN 0 7277 1695 6

Typeset by Pentacor PLC, High Wycombe, Bucks
Printed and bound in Great Britain by Spottiswoode Ballantyne Printers Ltd., Colchester

CONTENTS

ICE Conciliation Procedure: Included in looseleaf form in back cover flap

ICE Arbitration Procedure and ICE Arbitration Procedure (Scotland)
available from the publishers

CONTENTS OF ICE DESIGN AND CONSTRUCT CONDITIONS OF CONTRACT

MATERIALS AND WORKMANSHIP

COMMENCEMENT AND DELAYS

LIQUIDATED DAMAGES FOR DELAY

CERTIFICATE OF SUBSTANTIAL COMPLETION

OUTSTANDING WORK AND DEFECTS

ALTERATIONS AND ADDITIONAL PAYMENTS

MATERIALS AND CONTRACTOR'S EQUIPMENT

MEASUREMENT

PRIME COST ITEMS

CERTIFICATES AND PAYMENT

REMEDIES AND POWERS

SETTLEMENT OF DISPUTES

APPLICATION TO SCOTLAND ETC.

NOTICES

TAX MATTERS

SPECIAL CONDITIONS

INDEX

ICE Design and Construct Conditions of Contract

DEFINITIONS AND INTERPRETATION

Definitions   **1**   (1)   In the Contract (as hereinafter defined) the following words and expressions shall have the meanings hereby assigned to them except where the context otherwise requires.

(a) "Employer" means the person or persons firm company or other body named in the Appendix to the Form of Tender and includes the Employer's personal representatives successors and permitted assigns.

(b) "Contractor" means the person or persons firm or company to whom the Contract has been awarded by the Employer and includes the Contractor's personal representatives successors and permitted assigns.

(c) "Employer's Representative" means the person appointed by the Employer to act as such for the purposes of the Contract or any other person so appointed from time to time by the Employer and notified in writing as such to the Contractor.

(d) "Contractor's Representative" means the person appointed by the Contractor to act as such for the purposes of the Contract and notified in writing as such to the Employer or other person so appointed from time to time by the Contractor and similarly notified.

(e) "Employer's Requirements" means the requirements which are identified as such at the date of the award of the Contract and any subsequent variations thereto and which may describe the standards performance and/or objectives that are to be achieved by the Works or parts thereof.

(f) "Contractor's Submission" means the tender and all documents forming part of the Contractor's offer together with such modifications and additions thereto as may be agreed between the parties prior to the award of the Contract.

(g) "Contract" means the Conditions of Contract the Employer's Requirements the Contractor's Submission and the written acceptance thereof together with such other documents as may be expressly agreed between the parties and the Contract Agreement (if completed).

(h) "Contract Price" means the sum to be ascertained and paid for the design construction and completion of the Works in accordance with the Contract.

(i) "Prime Cost Item" means an item in the Contract which contains (either wholly or in part) a sum referred to as Prime Cost (PC) which will be used for the supply of goods materials or services for the Works.

(j) "Contingency" means any sum included and so designated in the Contract as a specific contingency for the carrying out of work or the supply of goods materials or services which may be used in whole in part or not at all in accordance with the specific requirements stated therefor.

1

(k) "Permanent Works" means the permanent works to be constructed and completed in accordance with the Contract.

(l) "Temporary Works" means all temporary works of every kind required in or about the construction and completion of the Works.

(m) "Works" means the Permanent Works and the Temporary Works and the design of both.

(n) "Commencement Date". As defined in Clause 41(1).

(o) "Certificate of Substantial Completion" means a certificate issued under Clause 48.

(p) "Defects Correction Period" means that period stated in the Appendix to the Form of Tender calculated from the date on which the Contractor becomes entitled to a Certificate of Substantial Completion for the Works or any Section or part thereof.

(q) "Defects Correction Certificate". As defined in Clause 61(1).

(r) "Section" means a part of the Works separately identified in the Appendix to the Form of Tender.

(s) "Site" means the lands and other places on under in or through which the Works are to be constructed and any other lands or places provided by the Employer for the purposes of the Contract together with such other places as may be designated in the Contract or subsequently agreed by the Employer's Representative as forming part of the Site.

(t) "Contractor's Equipment" means all appliances or things of whatever nature required in or about the construction and completion of the Works but does not include materials or other things intended to form or forming part of the Permanent Works.

Singular and plural

(2) Words importing the singular also include the plural and vice-versa where the context requires.

Headings and marginal notes

(3) The headings and marginal notes in the Conditions of Contract shall not be deemed to be part thereof or be taken into consideration in the interpretation or construction thereof or of the Contract.

Clause references

(4) All references herein to clauses are references to clauses numbered in the Conditions of Contract and not to those in any other document forming part of the Contract.

Cost

(5) The word "cost" when used in the Conditions of Contract means all expenditure including design costs properly incurred or to be incurred whether on or off the Site and overhead finance and other charges (including loss of interest) properly allocatable thereto but does not include any allowance for profit.

Communications in writing

(6) Communications which under the Contract are required to be "in writing" may be hand-written typewritten or printed and sent by hand post telex cable or facsimile.

Consent and approval

(7) (a) The giving of any consent or approval by or on behalf of the Employer's Representative shall not in any way relieve the Contractor of any of his obligations under the Contract or of his duty to ensure the correctness accuracy or suitability of the matter or thing which is the subject of the consent or approval.

(b) Failure by the Employer's Representative or any of his assistants to disapprove or object to any matter or thing shall not prejudice his power subsequently to take action under the Contract in connection therewith.

(c) Acceptance by the Employer's Representative of any programme or revised programme in accordance with Clause 14 shall not in any way imply that the programme so accepted is feasible suitable or appropriate and the Employer's rights under the Contract as to time shall in no way be impaired thereby.

EMPLOYER'S REPRESENTATIVE

Duties and authority of Employer's Representative

2 (1) (a) The Employer's Representative shall carry out the duties and may exercise the authority specified in or necessarily to be implied from the Contract.

(b) Except as expressly stated in the Contract the Employer's Representative shall have no authority to amend the Contract nor to relieve the Contractor of any of his obligations under the Contract.

Named individual

(2) Within 7 days of the award of the Contract and in any event before the Commencement Date the Employer shall notify to the Contractor in writing the name of the Employer's Representative. The Employer shall similarly notify the Contractor of any replacement of the Employer's Representative.

Delegation by the Employer's Representative

(3) The Employer's Representative may from time to time delegate to any person (including assistants appointed under sub-clause (4) of this Clause) any of the duties and authorities vested in him and he may at any time revoke such delegation.

Any such delegation

(a) shall be in writing and shall not take effect until such time as a copy thereof has been delivered to the Contractor or a representative appointed under Clause 15

(b) shall continue in force until such time as the Employer's Representative shall notify the Contractor or his representative in writing that the same has been revoked and

(c) shall not be given in respect of any decision to be taken or certificate to be issued under Clauses 12(6) 15(2)(b) 44 46(3) 48 60(4) 61 or 65.

Assistants

(4) (a) The Employer's Representative may appoint any number of assistants for the carrying out of his duties under the Contract . He shall notify to the Contractor the names duties and scope of authority of such assistants.

(b) Assistants may be appointed specifically to watch the construction of the Works.

(c) Assistants shall have no authority to relieve the Contractor of any of his duties or obligations under the Contract nor except as provided under sub-clause (3) of this Clause

(i) to order any work involving delay or any extra payment by the Employer or

(ii) to make any variation of or in the Works.

Instructions

(5) (a) Instructions given by the Employer's Representative or by any person exercising delegated duties and authorities under sub-clause (3) of this Clause shall be in writing. Provided that if for any reason

it is considered necessary to give any such instruction orally the Contractor shall comply therewith.

(b) Any such oral instruction shall be confirmed in writing by or on behalf of the Employer's Representative as soon as is possible in the circumstances. Provided that if the Contractor confirms in writing any such oral instruction which is not contradicted in writing by or on behalf of the Employer's Representative forthwith it shall be deemed to be an instruction in writing by the Employer's Representative.

(c) Upon the written request of the Contractor the Employer's Representative or the person exercising delegated duties or authorities under sub-clause (3) of this Clause shall specify in writing under which of his duties and authorities any instruction is given.

Reference on dissatisfaction

(6) If the Contractor is dissatisfied by reason of any act instruction or decision of any assistant appointed under this Clause he shall be entitled to refer the matter to the Employer's Representative for his decision.

ASSIGNMENT AND SUB-CONTRACTING

Assignment

3 Neither the Employer nor the Contractor shall assign the Contract or any part thereof or any benefit or interest therein or thereunder without the prior written consent of the other party which consent shall not unreasonably be withheld.

Sub-contracting

4 (1) The Contractor shall not sub-contract the whole of the construction of the Works without the prior written consent of the Employer.

(2) (a) The Contractor must obtain the Employer's consent prior to making any change in the Contractor's designer named in the Appendix to the Form of Tender which consent shall not unreasonably be withheld.

(b) Except where otherwise provided the Contractor may sub-contract any part of the construction of the Works. The extent of the work to be sub-contracted and the name and address of the sub-contractor must be notified in writing to the Employer's Representative prior to the sub-contractor's entry on to the Site.

(3) The employment of labour-only sub-contractors does not require notification to the Employer's Representative under sub-clause (2)(b) of this Clause.

(4) The Contractor shall be and remain liable under the Contract for all work sub-contracted and for acts defaults or neglects or any sub-contractor his agents servants or workpeople.

(5) The Employer's Representative may after due warning in writing require the Contractor to remove from the Works any sub-contractor who mis-conducts himself or is incompetent or negligent in the performance of his duties or fails to conform with any particular provisions with regard to safety which may be set out in the Contract or persists in any conduct which is prejudicial to safety or health and any such sub-contractor shall not be employed again upon the Works without the permission of the Employer's Representative.

DOCUMENTATION AND INFORMATION

Contract documents **5** (1) (a) The several documents forming the Contract are to be taken as mutually explanatory of one another.

(b) If in the light of the several documents forming the Contract there remain ambiguities or discrepancies between the Employer's Requirements and the Contractor's Submission the Employer's Requirements shall prevail.

(c) (i) Any ambiguities or discrepancies within the Employer's Requirements shall be explained and adjusted by the Employer's Representative who shall thereupon issue to the Contractor appropriate instructions in writing.

(ii) Should such instructions involve the Contractor in delay or disrupt his arrangements or methods of construction so as to cause him to incur cost beyond that reasonably to have been foreseen by an experienced contractor at the time of the award of the Contract then the Employer's Representative shall take such delay into account in determining any extension of time to which the Contractor is entitled under Clause 44 and the Contractor shall subject to Clause 53 be paid in accordance with Clause 60 the amount of such cost as may be reasonable. Profit shall be added thereto in respect of the design and construction of any additional permanent or temporary work.

(d) Any ambiguities or discrepancies within the Contractor's Submission shall be resolved at the Contractor's expense.

Supply of Contract documents (2) Upon the award of the Contract the Employer shall assemble two complete copies of the Contract of which one copy shall be supplied to the Contractor free of charge.

Further information **6** (1) (a) The Contractor shall give the Employer's Representative notice in writing of any further information from the Employer that is required for the design and/or construction of the Works and to which the Contractor is entitled under the Contract.

(b) Should the Employer's Representative fail to issue any such information within a reasonable period following notice he shall take that failure into account in determining any extension of time to which the Contractor is entitled under Clause 44 and the Contractor shall subject to Clause 53 be paid in accordance with Clause 60 any reasonable cost which may arise from the failure.

Designs and drawings (2) (a) The Contractor shall except as may otherwise be provided in the Contract submit to the Employer's Representative such designs and drawings as are necessary to show the general arrangement of the Works and that the Works will comply with the Employer's Requirements.

Construction to such designs and drawings shall not commence until the Employer's Representative has consented thereto.

(b) If in the opinion of the Employer's Representative any such design or drawing does not comply with the Employer's Requirements or with any other provision of the Contract he shall so inform the Contractor in writing giving his reasons and may withhold his consent thereto until the Contractor has re-submitted the design or drawing with appropriate modifications.

(c) The Contractor shall notify the Employer's Representative if he later wishes to modify any design or drawing to which consent has already been given and shall submit the modified design or drawing for further consent.

(d) Should the Employer's Representative fail within a reasonable period following the submission or re-submission of any design or drawing under this Clause to notify the Contractor either that he consents thereto or that he is withholding his consent he shall take such failure into account in determining any extension of time to which the Contractor is entitled under Clause 44 and the Contractor shall subject to Clause 53 be paid in accordance with Clause 60 any reasonable cost which may arise from such failure.

Supply of other information

(3) The Contractor shall supply to the Employer's Representative two copies of such other designs drawings specifications documents and information as the Employer's Representative may require.

Copyright

7 (1) (a) Copyright of all drawings specifications and other documents made by or on behalf of the Employer shall as between the parties remain in the Employer. The Contractor may obtain or make at his own expense any further copies required by him for the purposes of the Contract.

(b) Copyright of all drawings specifications and other documents made by or on behalf of the Contractor shall as between the parties remain in the Contractor. The Employer may obtain or make at his own expense any further copies required by him for the purposes of the Contract and after completion of the Works for the operation maintenance dismantling reassembly repair alteration and adjustment of the Permanent Works.

Documents to be available on Site

(2) One copy of the Contract and such further documents as may be consented to under Clause 6(2) and all working drawings shall be kept by the Contractor on Site and the same shall be available at all reasonable times for inspection and use by the Employer's Representative his assistants and any other person authorised by the Employer's Representative in writing.

GENERAL OBLIGATIONS

Contractor's general obligations

8 (1) The Contractor shall subject to the provisions of the Contract and save in so far as it is legally or physically impossible

(a) design construct and complete the Works and

(b) provide all design services labour materials Contractor's Equipment Temporary Works transport to and from and in or about the Site and everything whether of a temporary or permanent nature required in and for such design construction and completion so far as the necessity for providing the same is specified in or reasonably to be inferred from the Contract.

Contractor's design responsibility

(2) (a) In carrying out all his design obligations under the Contract including those arising under sub-clause (2)(b) of this Clause (and including the selection of materials and plant to the extent that these are not specified in the Employer's Requirements) the Contractor shall exercise all reasonable skill care and diligence.

(b) Where any part of the Works has been designed by or on behalf of the Employer and that design has been included in the Employer's Requirements the Contractor shall check the design and accept responsibility therefor having first obtained the approval of the Employer's Representative for any modifications thereto which the Contractor considers to be necessary.

Quality assurance

(3)   To the extent required by the Contract the Contractor shall institute a quality assurance system.

The Contractor's quality plan and procedures shall be submitted to the Employer's Representative for his prior approval before each design and each construction stage is commenced.

Should the Employer's Representative fail within a reasonable period following the Contractor's submission or re-submission of the quality plan and procedures to notify the Contractor either that he approves thereto or that he is withholding his approval he shall take such failure into account in determining any extension of time to which the Contractor is entitled under Clause 44 and the Contractor shall subject to Clause 53 be paid in accordance with Clause 60 any reasonable cost which may arise from such failure.

Compliance with such approved quality assurance system shall not relieve the Contractor from any of his other duties obligations or liabilities under the Contract.

Statutory checks

(4)   Where any Act of Parliament Regulation or Bye-law requires that a separate check of the design or a test shall be carried out prior to the construction or loading of any permanent and temporary works the Contractor shall arrange and pay for such check or test.

Contractor responsible for safety

(5)   The Contractor shall take responsibility for the safety of the design and for the adequacy stability and safety of all site operations and methods of construction.

Contract Agreement

9   The Contractor shall if called upon so to do enter into and execute a Contract Agreement to be prepared at the cost of the Employer in the form annexed to these Conditions.

Performance security

10   (1)   If the Contract requires the Contractor to provide security for the proper performance of the Contract he shall obtain and provide to the Employer within 28 days of the award of the Contract such security in a sum not exceeding 10% of the estimated total value of the Works at the date of the award of the Contract. The security shall be provided by a body approved by the Employer and be in the Form of Bond annexed to these Conditions. The Contractor shall pay the cost of the security unless the Contract otherwise provides.

Arbitration upon security

(2)   For the purposes of the arbitration provisions in such security

(a)   the Employer shall be deemed to be a party to the security for the purpose of doing everything necessary to give effect to such provisions and

(b)   any agreement decision award or other determination touching or concerning the relevant date for the discharge of the security shall be wholly without prejudice to the resolution or determination of any dispute between the Employer and the Contractor under Clause 66.

Provision and interpretation of information

11   (1)   The Employer shall be deemed to have made available to the Contractor before the submission of his tender all information on

(a)   the nature of the ground and subsoil including hydrological conditions and

(b)   pipes and cables in on or over the ground

obtained by or on behalf of the Employer from investigations undertaken relevant to the Works.

The Contractor shall be responsible for the interpretation of all such information for the purposes of the Works.

Inspection of Site

(2) The Contractor shall be deemed to have inspected and examined the Site and its surroundings and information available in connection therewith and to have satisfied himself so far as is practicable and reasonable before the award of the Contract as to

(a) the form and nature thereof including the ground and subsoil

(b) the extent and nature of work and materials necessary for constructing and completing the Works and

(c) the means of communication with and access to the Site and the accommodation he may require

and in general to **have** obtained for himself all necessary information as to risks contingencies and all other circumstances which may influence or affect his tender.

Basis and sufficiency of tender

(3) The Contractor shall be deemed to have

(a) based his tender on the information made available by the Employer and on his own inspection and examination all as aforementioned and

(b) satisfied himself before the Contract is awarded as to the correctness and sufficiency of the rates and/or prices stated therein which shall (unless otherwise provided in the Contract) cover all his obligations under the Contract.

Adverse physical conditions and artificial obstructions

12 (1) If during the carrying out of the Works the Contractor encounters physical conditions (other than weather conditions or conditions due to weather conditions) or artificial obstructions which conditions or obstructions could not in his opinion reasonably have been foreseen by an experienced contractor the Contractor shall as early as practicable give written notice thereof to the Employer's Representative.

(2) If in addition the Contractor intends to make any claim for additional payment or extension of time arising from any such condition or obstruction he shall at the same time or as soon thereafter as may be reasonable inform the Employer's Representative in writing pursuant to Clause 53 and/or Clause 44(1) as may be appropriate specifying the condition or obstruction to which the claim relates.

Measures being taken

(3) When giving notification in accordance with sub-clauses (1) and/or (2) of this Clause or as soon as practicable thereafter the Contractor shall give details of any anticipated effects of the condition or obstruction the measures he has taken is taking or is proposing to take their estimated cost and the extent of the anticipated delay in or interference with the carrying out of the Works. Such details shall include where appropriate consideration of alternative measures and/or methods of procedure with comparative estimates of costs and delays.

Action by Employer's Representative

(4) Following receipt of any notification under sub-clauses (1) (2) or (3) of this Clause The Employer's Representative may if he thinks fit *inter alia*

(a) give written consent to any measures with or without modification or

(b) order a suspension under Clause 40 or issue a variation order under Clause 51.

Conditions reasonably foreseeable

(5) If the Employer's Representative decides that any such condition or obstruction could in whole or in part have been reasonably foreseen by an experienced contractor he shall so inform the Contractor in writing as soon as he has reached that decision but the value of any variation previously ordered by him pursuant to sub-clause (4)(b) of this Clause shall be ascertained in accordance with Clause 52 and paid for in accordance with Clause 60.

Delay and extra cost

(6) Where any claim is made pursuant to sub-clause (2) of this Clause and if in his opinion any such condition or obstruction could not reasonably have been foreseen by an experienced contractor the Employer's Representative shall

(a) determine the reasonable cost of carrying out any additional work and of using any additional Contractor's Equipment which would not have been needed had the condition or obstruction not been encountered together with a reasonable percentage addition thereto in respect of profit and shall notify the Contractor accordingly with a copy to the Employer and

(b) take any delay suffered by the Contractor as a result of the condition or obstruction into account in determining any extension of time to which the Contractor is entitled under Clause 44.

The Contractor shall subject to Clause 53 be paid in accordance with Clause 60 both the amount so determined and the reasonable cost of any delay or disruption to the rest of the Works.

13 Not used.

Programme to be furnished

14 (1) (a) Within 21 days after the award of the Contract the Contractor shall submit to the Employer's Representative for his acceptance a programme showing the order in which he proposes to carry out the Works having regard to the provisions of Clause 42(1).

(b) At the same time the Contractor shall also provide in writing for the information of the Employer's Representative a general description of the arrangements and methods of construction which the Contractor proposes to adopt for the carrying out of the Works.

(c) Should the Employer's Representative reject any programme under sub-clause (2)(b) of this Clause the Contractor shall within 21 days of such rejection submit a revised programme.

Action by Employer's Representative

(2) The Employer's Representative shall within 21 days after receipt of the Contractor's programme

(a) accept the programme in writing or

(b) reject the programme in writing with reasons or

(c) request the Contractor to supply further information to clarify or substantiate the programme or to satisfy the Employer's Representative as to its reasonableness having regard to the Contractor's obligations under the Contract.

Provided that if none of the above actions is taken within the said period of 21 days the Employer's Representative shall be deemed to have accepted the programme as submitted.

Further information

(3) The Contractor shall within 21 days after receiving from the Employer's Representative any request under sub-clause (2)(c) of this

Clause or within such further period as the Employer's Representative may allow provide the further information requested failing which the relevant programme shall be deemed to be rejected.

Upon receipt of such further information the Employer's Representative shall within a further 21 days accept or reject the programme in accordance with sub-clauses (2)(a) or (2)(b) of this Clause.

Revision of programme

(4)   Should it appear to the Employer's Representative at any time that the actual progress of the work does not conform with the accepted programme referred to in sub-clauses (2) or (3) of this Clause the Employer's Representative shall be entitled to require the Contractor to produce a revised programme showing such modification to that programme as may be necessary to ensure completion of the Works or any Section within the time for completion as defined in Clause 43 or extended time granted pursuant to Clause 44.

In such event the Contractor shall submit his revised programme within 21 days or within such further period as the Employer's Representative may allow. Thereafter the provisions of sub-clauses (2) and (3) of this Clause shall apply.

Design criteria

(5)   The Employer's Representative shall provide to the Contractor such design criteria relevant to the Employer's Requirements as may be necessary to enable the Contractor to comply with sub-clause (6) of this Clause.

Methods of construction

(6)   If requested by the Employer's Representative the Contractor shall submit at such times and in such further detail as the Employer's Representative may reasonably require information pertaining to the design and methods of construction (including Temporary Works and the use of Contractor's Equipment) which the Contractor proposes to adopt or use together with calculations of stresses strains and deflections that will arise in the Permanent Works or any parts thereof during construction so as to demonstrate to the Employer's Representative that if these methods are adhered to the Works can be constructed and completed in accordance with the Contract and without detriment to the Permanent Works when completed.

Contractor's superintendence

15   (1)   The Contractor shall provide all necessary superintendence during the carrying out of the Works and for as long thereafter as the Employer's Representative may reasonably consider necessary.

Such superintendence shall be given by sufficient persons having adequate knowledge of the operations to be carried out (including the methods and techniques required the hazards likely to be encountered and methods of preventing accidents) for the satisfactory and safe carrying out of the Works.

Contractor's Representative

(2)   (a)   The Contractor's Representative shall exercise overall superintendence of the Works on behalf of the Contractor. He shall receive on behalf of the Contractor all consents approvals orders instructions and information given by the Employer's Representative.

The Contractor's Representative shall have the authority to act and to commit the Contractor as if he were the Contractor for the purposes of the Contract.

(b)   The Contractor's Representative may delegate any of his responsibilities to a nominated deputy with the prior written agreement of the Employer's Representative. Information and decisions from any such nominated deputy shall be as if from the Contractor's Representative.

Contractor's agent

(3) The Contractor's Representative or a competent and authorized agent approved in writing by the Employer's Representative (which approval may at any time be withdrawn) shall superintend the construction of the Permanent and Temporary Works.

From the time that the Contractor commences work on Site the authorized agent

(a) shall give his whole time to such superintendence

(b) shall receive on behalf of the Contractor any consents approvals orders instructions and information from any of the assistants of the Employer's Representative and

(c) may also receive on behalf of the Contractor's Representative consents approvals orders instructions and information from the Employer's Representative.

Removal of Contractor's employees

16 (1) The Contractor shall employ or cause to be employed in connection with the Works and in the superintendence thereof only persons who are careful skilled and experienced in their several professions trades and callings.

(2) The Employer's Representative shall be at liberty to object to and require the Contractor to remove or cause to be removed from the Works any person employed thereon who in the opinion of the Employer's Representative misconducts himself or is incompetent or negligent in the performance of his duties or fails to conform with any particular provisions with regard to safety which may be set out in the Contract or persists in any conduct which is prejudicial to safety or health and such persons shall not be employed again upon the Works without the permission of the Employer's Representative.

17 Not used.

Boreholes and exploratory excavation

18 (1) If during the performance of the Works the Contractor considers it necessary or desirable to make boreholes or to carry out exploratory excavations or investigations of the ground he shall apply to the Employer's Representative for permission so to do giving his reasons and details of his proposed methods. Such permission shall not unreasonably be withheld.

The Contractor shall comply with any conditions imposed by the Employer's Representative in relation thereto and shall furnish the Employer's Representative with copies of all information records and test results arising therefrom and of any expert opinion as may be provided in connection therewith.

(2) The cost of making such boreholes and carrying out such investigations and of all other matters connected therewith including making good thereafter to the satisfaction of the Employer's Representative shall be borne by the Contractor. Provided that if in the opinion of the Employer's Representative the boreholes excavations and investigations are a necessary consequence of

(a) a situation arising under Clause 12 they shall be paid for in accordance with that Clause or

(b) a variation ordered under Clause 51 they shall for the purposes of payment be treated as part of that variation and priced in accordance with Clause 52.

(3) If during the performance of the Works the Employer's Representative requires the Contractor to make boreholes or to carry out

exploratory excavations or investigations of the ground such requirements shall be ordered in writing and shall be deemed to be a variation
ordered under Clause 51 unless a Contingency or Prime Cost Item in
respect of such anticipated work is included in the Contract.

Safety and security   **19**   (1)   The Contractor shall throughout the progress of the Works have
full regard for the safety of all persons entitled to be upon the Site and
shall keep the Site (so far as the same is under his control) and the Works
(so far as the same are not completed or occupied by the Employer) in an
orderly state appropriate to the avoidance of danger to such persons and
shall *inter alia* in connection with the Works provide and maintain at his
own cost all lights guards fencing warning signs and watching when and
where necessary or required by the Employer's Representative or any of
his assistants or by any competent statutory or other authority for the
protection of the Works or for the safety and convenience of the public or
others.

Employer's responsibilities   (2)   If under Clause 31 the Employer carries out work on the Site with
his own workpeople he shall in respect of such work

(a)   have full regard for the safety of all persons entitled to be on
the Site and

(b)   keep the Site in an orderly state appropriate to the avoidance
of danger to such persons.

If under Clause 31 the Employer employs other contractors on the Site he
shall require them to have the same regard for safety and avoidance of
danger.

Care of the Works   **20**   (1)   (a)   The Contractor shall save as in paragraph (b) hereof and
subject to sub-clause (2) of this Clause take full responsibility for
the care of the Works and for materials plant and equipment for
incorporation therein from the Commencement Date until the date
of issue of a Certificate of Substantial Completion for the whole of
the Works when the responsibility for the said care shall pass to the
Employer.

(b)   If the Employer's Representative issues a Certificate of
Substantial Completion for any Section or part of the Permanent
Works the Contractor shall cease to be responsible for the care of
that Section or part from the date of issue of that Certificate of
Substantial Completion when the responsibility for the care of that
Section or part shall pass to the Employer. Provided always that the
Contractor shall remain responsible for any damage to such
completed work caused by or as a result of his other activities on the
Site.

(c)   The Contractor shall take full responsibility for the care of any
outstanding work and materials plant and equipment for incorporation therein which he undertakes to finish during the Defects
Correction Period until such outstanding work has been completed.

Excepted Risks   (2)   Risks for which the Contractor is not liable are loss and damage to
the extent that they are due to

(a)   the use or occupation by the Employer his agents servants or
other contractors (not being employed by the Contractor) of any
part of the Permanent Works

(b)   any fault defect error or omission in the design of the Works
for which the Contractor is not responsible under the Contract

(c)   riot war invasion act of foreign enemies or hostilities (whether
war be declared or not)

(d) civil war rebellion revolution insurrection or military or usurped power

(e) ionizing radiations or contamination by radioactivity from any nuclear fuel or from any nuclear waste from the combustion of nuclear fuel radioactive toxic explosive or other hazardous properties of any explosive nuclear assembly or nuclear component thereof and

(f) pressure waves caused by aircraft or other aerial devices travelling at sonic or supersonic speeds.

Rectification of loss or damage

(3) (a) In the event of any loss or damage to

(i) the Works or any Section or part thereof or

(ii) materials plant or equipment for incorporation therein

while the Contractor is responsible for the care thereof (except as provided in sub-clause (2) of this Clause) the Contractor shall at his own cost rectify such loss or damage so that the Permanent Works conform in every respect with the provisions of the Contract. The Contractor shall also be liable for any loss or damage to the Works occasioned by him in the course of any operations carried out by him for the purpose of complying with his obligations under Clauses 49 and 50

(b) Should any loss or damage arise from any of the Excepted Risks defined in sub-clause (2) of this Clause the Contractor shall if and to the extent required by the Employer' Representative rectify the loss or damage at the expense of the Employer.

(c) In the event of loss or damage arising from an Excepted Risk and a risk for which the Contractor is responsible under sub-clause (1)(a) of this Clause then the cost of rectification shall be apportioned accordingly.

insurance of Permanent and Temporary Works etc.

21 (1) The Contractor shall without limiting his or the Employer's obligations and responsibilities under Clause 20 insure in the joint names of the Contractor and the Employer the Permanent and Temporary Works together with materials plant and equipment for incorporation therein to the full replacement cost plus an additional 10% to cover any additional costs that may arise incidental to the rectification of any loss or damage including professional fees cost of demolition and removal of debris.

Extent of cover

(2) (a) The insurance required under sub-clause (1) of this Clause shall cover the Employer and the Contractor against all loss or damage from whatsoever cause arising other than the Excepted Risks defined in Clause 20(2) from the Commencement Date until the date of issue of the relevant Certificate of Substantial Completion.

(b) The insurance shall extend to cover any loss or damage arising during the Defects Correction Period from a cause occurring prior to the issue of any Certificate of Substantial Completion and any loss or damage occasioned by the Contractor in the course of any operation carried out by him for the purpose of complying with his obligations under Clauses 49 and 50.

(c) Nothing in this Clause shall render the Contractor liable to insure against the necessity for the repair or reconstruction of any work constructed with materials or workmanship not in accordance with the requirements of the Contract unless the Contract otherwise requires.

(d) Any amounts not insured or not recovered from insurers whether as excesses carried under the policy or otherwise shall be borne by the Contractor or the Employer in accordance with their respective responsibilities under Clause 20.

Damage to persons or property

22 (1) The Contractor shall except if and so far as the Contract provides otherwise and subject to the exceptions set out in sub-clause (2) of this Clause indemnify and keep indemnified the Employer against all losses and claims in respect of

(a) death of or injury to any person or

(b) loss of or damage to any property (other than the Works)

which may arise out of or in consequence of the design construction and completion of the Works and the remedying of any defects therein and against all claims demands proceedings damages costs charges and expenses whatsoever in respect thereof or in relation thereto.

Exceptions

(2) The exceptions referred to in sub-clause (1) of this Clause which are the responsibility of the Employer are

(a) damage to crops being on the Site (save in so far as possession has not been given to the Contractor)

(b) the use or occupation of land provided by the Employer for the purposes of the Contract (including consequent losses of crops) or interference whether temporary or permanent with any right of way light air or water or other easement or quasi-easement which is the unavoidable result of the construction of the Works in accordance with the Contract

(c) the right of the Employer to construct the Works or any part thereof on over under in or through any land

(d) damage which is the unavoidable result of the construction of the Works in accordance with the Employer's Requirements including any design for which the Contractor is not responsible under the Contract and

(e) death of or injury to persons or loss of or damage to property resulting from any act neglect or breach of statutory duty done or committed by the Employer his agents servants or other contractors (not being employed by the Contractor) or for or in respect of any claims demands proceedings damages costs charges and expenses in respect thereof or in relation thereto.

Indemnity by Employer

(3) The Employer shall subject to sub-clause (4) of this Clause indemnify the Contractor against all claims demands proceedings damages costs charges and expenses in respect of the matters referred to in the exceptions defined in sub-clause (2) of this Clause.

Shared responsibility

(4) (a) The Contractor's liability to indemnify the Employer under sub-clause (1) of this Clause shall be reduced in proportion to the extent that the act or neglect of the Employer his agents servants or other contractors (not being employed by the Contractor) may have contributed to the said death injury loss or damage.

(b) The Employers liability to indemnify the Contractor under sub-clause (3) of this Clause in respect of matters referred to in sub-clause (2)(e) of this Clause shall be reduced in proportion to the extent that the act or neglect of the Contractor or his sub-contractors servants or agents may have contributed to the said death injury loss or damage.

14

Third party insurance 23 (1) The Contractor shall without limiting his or the Employer's obligations and responsibilities under Clause 22 insure in the joint names of the Contractor and the Employer against liabilities for death of or injury to any person (other than any operative or other person in the employment of the Contractor or any of his sub-contractors) or loss of or damage to any property (other than the Works) arising out of the performance of the Contract other than those due to the exceptions defined in Clause 22 (2) (a)(b)(c) and (d).

(2) The insurance policy shall include a cross liability clause such that the insurance shall apply to the Contractor and to the Employer as separate insured.

(3) Such insurance shall be for at least the amount stated in the Appendix to the Form of Tender.

Accident or injury to workpeople 24 The Employer shall not be liable for or in respect of any damages or compensation payable at law in respect or in consequence of any accident or injury to any operative or other person in the employment of the Contractor or any of his sub-contractors save and except and to the extent that such accident or injury results from or is contributed to by any act or default of the Employer his agents or servants and the Contractor shall indemnify and keep indemnified the Employer against all such damages and compensation (save and except as aforesaid) and against all claims demands proceedings costs charges and expenses whatsoever in respect thereof or in relation thereto.

Evidence and terms of Insurance 25 (1) The Contractor shall provide satisfactory evidence to the Employer prior to the Commencement Date that the insurances required under the Contract have been effected and shall if so required produce the insurance policies for inspection. The terms of all such insurances shall be subject to the approval of the Employer (which approval shall not unreasonably be withheld). The Contractor shall upon request produce to the Employer receipts for the payment of current insurance premiums.

Excesses (2) Any excesses on the policies of insurance effected under Clauses 21 and 23 shall be as stated by the Contractor in the Appendix to the Form of Tender.

Remedy on Contractor's failure to insure (3) If the Contractor fails upon request to produce to the Employer satisfactory evidence that there is in force any of the insurances required under the Contract then the Employer may effect and keep in force any such insurance and pay such premium or premiums as may be necessary for that purpose and from time to time deduct the amount so paid from any monies due or which may become due to the Contractor or recover the same as a debt due from the Contractor.

Compliance with policy conditions (4) Both the Employer and the Contractor shall comply with all conditions laid down in the insurance policies. Should the Contractor or the Employer fail to comply with any condition imposed by the insurance policies effected pursuant to the Contract each shall indemnify the other against all losses and claims arising from such failure.

Giving of notices and payment of fees 26 (1) The Contractor shall save as provided in sub-clause (3)(d) of this Clause give all notices and pay all fees required to be given or paid by any Act of Parliament or any Regulation or Bye-law of any local or other statutory authority in relation to the design construction and completion of the Permanent Works and the Temporary Works and by the rules and regulations of all public bodies and companies whose property or rights are or may be affected in any way by the Works.

Repayment by Employer

(2)   The Employer shall repay or allow to the Contractor all such sums as the Employer's Representative certifies to have been properly payable and paid by the Contractor in respect of such fees and and also all rates and taxes paid by the Contractor in respect of the Site or any part thereof or anything constructed or erected thereon or any part thereof or any temporary structures situated elsewhere but used exclusively for the purpose of the Works or any structures used temporarily and exclusively for the purposes of the Works.

Contractor to conform with Statutes etc.

(3)   The Contractor shall ascertain and conform in all respects with the provisions of any general or local Act of Parliament and the Regulations and Bye-laws of any local or other statutory authority which may be applicable to the Works and with such rules and regulations of public bodies and companies as aforesaid and shall keep the Employer indemnified against all penalties and liability of every kind for breach of any Act Regulation or Bye-law.

Provided always that

(a)   the Contractor shall not be required to indemnify the Employer against the consequences of any such breach which is the unavoidable result of complying with the Contract or instructions of the Employer's Representative

(b)   if the Employer's Requirements are at any time found to preclude conformity with any such Act Regulation or Bye-law the Employer's Representative shall issue such instructions including the ordering of a variation under Clause 51 as may be necessary to ensure conformity with such Act Regulation or Bye-law

(c)   unless the Contract otherwise provides the Contractor shall not be responsible for obtaining any planning permission which may be necessary in respect of the Permanent Works or of any Temporary Works designed other than by or on behalf of the Contractor and the Employer shall be deemed to warrant that all such permissions have been or will in due time be obtained and

(d)   unless the Contract otherwise provides the Contractor shall be responsible for the service of notices under the New Roads and Street Works Act 1991 after the award of the Contract.

27   Not used.

Patent rights   28   (1)   The Contractor shall save harmless and indemnify the Employer from and against all claims and proceedings for or on account of infringement of any patent right design trademark or name or other protected right in respect of

(a)   the design construction and completion of the Works or any part thereof or

(b)   any Contractor's Equipment used for or in connection with the Works or

(c)   any materials plant or equipment for incorporation in the Works and from and against all claims demands proceedings damages costs charges and expenses whatsoever in respect thereof or in relation thereto except as provided in sub-clause (2) of this Clause.

(2)   In like manner the Employer shall save harmless and indemnify the Contractor

(a)   where such infringement results from compliance with any design or specification provided other than by or on behalf of the Contractor or

(b) where the infringement is due to the use of the Works or any part thereof in association or in combination with any artifact not supplied by or on behalf of the Contractor or

(c) where the infringement is due to the use of the Works (whether by the Employer or some other person or legal entity having the lawful use thereof) other than for a purpose indicated by or reasonably to be inferred from the Employer's Requirements

from and against all claims and proceedings for or on account of such infringement and from and against all claims demands proceedings damages costs charges and expenses whatsoever in respect thereof or in relation thereto.

Royalties

(3) The Contractor shall pay all tonnage and other royalties rent and other payments or compensation (if any) for getting stone sand gravel clay or other materials required for the Works.

Interference with traffic and adjoining properties

29 (1) All operations necessary for the construction and completion of the Works shall so far as compliance with the requirements of the Contract permits be carried on so as not to interfere unnecessarily or improperly with

(a) the convenience of the public or

(b) the access to public or private roads footpaths or properties whether in the possession of the Employer or of any other person and with the use or occupation thereof.

The Contractor shall save harmless and indemnify the Employer in respect of all claims demands proceedings damages costs charges and expenses whatsoever arising out of or in relation to any such matters.

Noise disturbance and pollution

(2) All work shall be carried out without unreasonable noise disturbance or other pollution.

Indemnity by Contractor

(3) To the extent that noise disturbance or other pollution is not the unavoidable consequence of constructing and completing the Works or performing the Contract the Contractor shall indemnify the Employer from and against any liability for damages on that account and against all claims demands proceedings damages costs charges and expenses whatsoever in regard or in relation to such liability

Indemnity by Employer

(4) The Employer shall indemnify the Contractor from and against any liability for damages on account of noise disturbance or other pollution which is the unavoidable consequence of carrying out the Permanent and Temporary Works and from and against all claims demands proceedings damages costs charges and expenses whatsoever in regard or in relation to such liability.

Avoidance of damage to highways etc.

30 (1) The Contractor shall use every reasonable means to prevent any of the highways or bridges communicating with or on the routes to the Site from being subjected to extraordinary traffic within the meaning of the Highways Act 1980 or in Scotland the Roads (Scotland) Act 1984 or any statutory modification or re-enactment thereof by any traffic of the Contractor or any of his sub-contractors.

In particular the Contractor shall select routes and use vehicles and restrict and distribute loads so that any such extraordinary traffic as will inevitably arise from the moving of Contractor's Equipment and materials or manufactured or fabricated articles from and to the Site shall be limited as far as reasonably possible and so that no unnecessary damage or injury may be occasioned to such highways and bridges.

Transport of Contractor's Equipment

(2) Save in so far as the Contract otherwise provides the Contractor shall be responsible for and shall pay the cost of strengthening any bridges or altering or improving any highway communicating with the Site to facilitate the movement of Contractor's Equipment or Temporary Works or materials therefor required in the construction and completion of the Works.

The Contractor shall indemnify and keep indemnified the Employer against all claims for damage to any highway or bridge communicating with the Site caused by such movement including such claims as may be made by any competent authority directly against the Employer pursuant to any Act of Parliament or other Statutory Instrument and shall negotiate and pay all claims arising solely out of such damage.

Transport of materials

(3) (a) If notwithstanding sub-clause (1) of this Clause any damage occurs to any bridge or highway communicating with the Site arising from the transport of materials or manufactured or fabricated articles being part of the Permanent Works the Contractor shall notify the Employer's Representative as soon as he becomes aware of such damage or as soon as he receives any claim from the authority entitled to make such a claim.

(b) Where under any Act of Parliament or Statutory Instrument the haulier of such materials or manufactured or fabricated articles is required to indemnify the highway authority against damage the Employer shall not be liable for any costs charges or expenses in respect thereof or in relation thereto.

(c) In all cases under this sub-clause other than those covered in paragraph (b) hereof the Employer shall negotiate the settlement of and pay all sums due in respect of such claims and shall indemnify the Contractor in respect thereof and in respect of all claims demands proceedings damages costs charges and expenses in relation thereto.

Provided always that if and so far as any such claim or part thereof is in the opinion of the Employer's Representative due to any failure on the part of the Contractor to observe and perform his obligations under sub-clause (1) of this Clause then the amount certified by the Employer's Representative to be due to such failure shall be paid by the Contractor to the Employer or deducted from any sum due or which may become due to the Contractor.

Facilities for other contractors   31

(1) The Contractor shall in accordance with the requirements of the Employer's Representative afford all reasonable facilities for any other contractors employed by the Employer and for the employees of the Employer and of any other properly authorized authorities or statutory bodies who may be employed in carrying out on or near the Site any work not in the Contract.

Delay and extra cost

(2) If compliance with sub-clause (1) of this Clause involves the Contractor in delay or cost beyond that reasonably to be foreseen by an experienced contractor at the date of award of the Contract then the Employer's Representative shall take such delay into account in determining any extension of time to which the Contractor is entitled under Clause 44 and the Contractor shall subject to Clause 53 be paid in accordance with Clause 60 the amount of such cost as may be reasonable. Profit shall be added thereto in respect of any additional permanent or temporary work.

Fossils etc.   32

All fossils coins articles of value or antiquity and structures or other remains or things of geological or archaeological interest discovered on the Site shall as between the Employer and the Contractor be deemed to be the absolute property of the Employer and the Contractor shall take reasonable precautions to prevent his employees or any other person from removing or damaging any such article or thing and shall immediately upon discovery thereof and before removal inform the Employer's Representative of such discovery and carry out at the expense of the Employer the Employer's Representative's orders as to the examination and disposal of the same.

Clearance of Site on completion 33 (1) On completion of the Works the Contractor shall clear away and remove from the Site all Contractor's Equipment surplus material rubbish and Temporary Works of any kind and leave the whole of the Site and Permanent Works clean and in workmanlike condition to the satisfaction of the Employer's Representative.

Disposal of Contractor's Equipment (2) If the Contractor fails to remove any Contractor's Equipment Temporary Works goods or materials as required by sub-clause (1) of this Clause within such reasonable time after completion of the Works as the Employer's Representative may allow then the Employer may sell or otherwise dispose of such items. From the proceeds of the sale of any such items the Employer shall be entitled to retain any costs or expenses incurred in connection with their sale and/or disposal before paying the balance (if any) to the Contractor.

34 Not used.

Returns of labour and Contractor's Equipment 35 (1) If the Contract so provides the Contractor shall deliver to the Employer's Representative a return in such form and at such intervals as the Employer's Representative may prescribe showing in detail the numbers of the several classes of labour from time to time employed by the Contractor on the Site and such information in respect of Contractor's Equipment as the Employer's Representative may require. The Contractor shall require his sub-contractors to observe the provisions of this Clause.

(2) If the Contract contains no such provision the Contractor shall nevertheless and if so requested in writing by the Employer's Representative deliver a return in like manner in connection with any variation claim or event.

MATERIALS AND WORKMANSHIP

Materials and workmanship 36 (1) The Works shall be designed constructed and completed in accordance with the Contract and where not expressly provided otherwise in the Contract in accordance with appropriate standards and standard codes of practice.

(2) All materials and workmanship shall be of the respective kinds described in the Contract or where not so described shall be appropriate in all the circumstances.

Checks and tests (3) (a) Further to his obligations under Clause 8(3) the Contractor shall submit to the Employer's Representative for his approval proposals for checking the design and setting out of the Works and testing the materials and workmanship to ensure that the Contractor's obligations under the Contract are met.

(b) The Contractor shall carry out the checks and tests approved under sub-clause (3)(a) of this Clause or elsewhere in the Contract and such further tests as the Employer's Representative may reasonably require.

Tests

(4)   The Contractor shall provide such assistance and such instruments machines labour and materials as are normally required for examining measuring and testing any work and the quality weight or quantity of any materials used and shall supply samples of materials before incorporation in the Works for testing as may be required by the Employer's Representative.

Cost of samples

(5)   All samples shall be supplied by the Contractor at his own cost if the supply thereof is clearly intended by or provided for in the Contract but if not then at the cost of the Employer.

Tests following variations

(6)   Whenever a variation is ordered or consented to by the Employer's Representative the Contractor shall consider whether any tests would be affected by or be appropriate in relation thereto and shall so inform the Employer' Representative without delay. Any proposal for amended or additional tests shall be submitted as soon as possible.

Cost of tests

(7)   Unless the Contract otherwise provides the cost of making any test shall be borne by the Contractor if such test is

(a)   proposed by the Contractor under Clause 8(3) or sub-clause (3)(a) of this Clause or

(b)   clearly intended by or provided for in the Contract.

If any test is carried out pursuant to sub-clause (3)(b) of this Clause the cost of such test shall be borne by the Contractor if the test shows the workmanship or materials not to be in accordance with the provisions of the Contract but otherwise by the Employer.

Access to site   **37**   The Employer's Representative and any person authorized by him shall at all times have access to the Works and to the Site and to all workshops and places where work is being prepared or whence materials manufactured articles and machinery are being obtained for the Works and the Contractor shall afford every facility for and every assistance in obtaining such access or the right to such access.

Examination of work before covering up   **38**   (1)   The Contractor shall afford full opportunity for the Employer's Representative to examine and measure any work which is about to be covered up or put out of view and to examine foundations before permanent work is placed thereon.

The Contractor shall give due notice to the Employer's Representative whenever any such work or foundations is or are ready or about to be ready for examination and the Employer's Representative shall without unreasonable delay attend for the purpose of examining and measuring such work or of examining such foundations unless he considers it unnecessary and advises the Contractor accordingly.

Uncovering and making openings

(2)   The Contractor shall uncover any part or parts of the Works or make openings in or through the same as the Employer's Representative may from time to time direct and shall reinstate and make good such part or parts to the satisfaction of the Employer's Representative.

If any such part or parts have been covered up or put out of view after compliance with the requirements of sub-clause (1) of this Clause and are found to have been carried out in accordance with the Contract the cost of uncovering making openings in or through reinstating and making good the same shall be borne by the Employer but in any other case all such cost shall be borne by the Contractor.

Removal of unsatisfactory work and materials

39 The Employer's Representative shall during the progress of the Works have power to instruct in writing

(a) the removal from the Site within such time or times specified in the instruction of any materials which in the opinion of the Employer's Representative do not comply with the Contract

(b) the replacement of such materials with others that do so comply and

(c) the removal and proper replacement (notwithstanding any previous test thereof or interim payment therefor) of any work which in respect of

(i) materials or workmanship or

(ii) design by the Contractor or for which he is responsible

does not in the opinion of the Employer's Representative comply with the Contract.

Suspension of Works

40 (1) The Contractor shall on the written order of the Employer's Representative suspend the progress of the Works or any part thereof for such time or times and in such manner as the Employer's Representative may consider necessary and shall during such suspension properly protect and secure any work so far as is necessary in the opinion of the Employer's Representative.

Subject to Clause 53 the Contractor shall be paid in accordance with Clause 60 the extra cost (if any) incurred in giving effect to the Employer's Representative's instructions under this Clause except to the extent that such suspension is

(a) otherwise provided for in the Contract or

(b) necessary by reason of weather conditions or by some default on the part of the Contractor or

(c) necessary for the proper construction and completion or for the safety of the Works or any part thereof in as much as such necessity does not arise from any act or default of the Employer's Representative or the Employer or from any of the Excepted Risks defined in Clause 20(2).

Profit shall be added thereto in respect of any additional permanent or temporary work.

The Employer's Representative shall take any delay occasioned by a suspension order under this Clause (including that arising from any act or default of the Employer's Representative or the Employer) into account in determining any extension of time to which the Contractor is entitled under Clause 44 except when such suspension is otherwise provided for in the Contract or is necessary by reason of some default on the part of the Contractor.

Suspension lasting more than three months

(2) If the progress of the Works or any part thereof is suspended on the written order of the Employer's Representative and if permission to resume work is not given by the Employer's Representative within a period of 3 months from the date of suspension then the Contractor may unless such suspension is otherwise provided for in the Contract or continues to be necessary by reason of some default on the part of the Contractor serve a written notice on the Employer's Representative requiring permission within 28 days from the receipt of such notice to proceed with the Works or that part thereof in regard to which progress is suspended.

If within the said 28 days the Employer's Representative does not grant such permission the Contractor by a further written notice so served may elect to treat the suspension where it affects part only of the Works as an omission of such part under Clause 51 or where it affects the whole of the Works as an abandonment of the Contract by the Employer.

COMMENCEMENT AND DELAYS

Commencement Date 41 (1) The Commencement Date shall be

(a) the date specified in the Appendix to the Form of Tender or if no date is specified

(b) such other date as may be agreed between the parties or in default of agreement

(c) 28 days after the award of the Contract.

Start of Works (2) The Contractor shall start the Works on or as soon as is reasonably practicable after the Commencement Date. Thereafter the Contractor shall proceed therewith with due expedition and without delay in accordance with the Contract.

Possession of Site and access 42 (1) The Contract may prescribe

(a) the extent of portions of the Site of which the Contractor is to be given possession from time to time

(b) the order in which such portions of the Site shall be made available to the Contractor

(c) the availability and the nature of the access which is to be provided by the Employer and

(d) the order in which the Works shall be constructed.

(2) (a) Subject to sub-clause (1) of this Clause the Employer shall give to the Contractor on the Commencement Date possession of so much of the Site and access thereto as may be required to enable the Contractor to commence and proceed with the Works.

(b) Thereafter the Employer shall during the course of the Works give the Contractor possession of such further portions of the Site as may be required in accordance with the programme which the Employer's Representative has accepted under Clause 14 and such further access as is necessary to enable the Contractor to proceed with the Works with due despatch.

Failure to give possession (3) If the Contractor suffers delay and/or incurs additional cost from failure on the part of the Employer to give possession in accordance with the terms of this Clause the Employer's Representative shall determine

(a) any extension of time to which the Contractor is entitled under Clause 44 and

(b) subject to Clause 53 the amount of any additional cost to which the Contractor may be entitled together with profit thereon in respect of any additional permanent or temporary work

and shall notify the Contractor accordingly with a copy to the Employer. The Contractor shall thereupon be paid in accordance with Clause 60 the amount so determined.

Access and facilities provided by the Contractor

(4)   The Contractor shall bear all costs and char_ required by him additional to that provided by th_ Contractor shall also provide at his own cost any a_ outside the Site required by him for the purposes of the ˋ

Time for completion   **43**   The whole of the Works and any Section required to be c_ a particular time as stated in the Appendix to the Form of substantially completed within the time so stated (or such ...ended time as may be allowed under Clause 44) calculated from the Commencement Date.

Extension of time for completion   **44**   (1)   Should the Contractor consider that

(a)   any variation ordered under Clause 51(1) or

(b)   any cause of delay referred to in these Conditions or

(c)   exceptional adverse weather conditions or

(d)   other special circumstances of any kind whatsoever which may occur

be such as to entitle him to an extension of time for the substantial completion of the Works or any Section thereof he shall within 28 days after the cause of any delay has arisen or as soon thereafter as is reasonable deliver to the Employer's Representative full and detailed particulars in justification of the period of extension claimed in order that the claim may be investigated at the time.

Assessment of delay

(2)   (a) The Employer's Representative shall upon receipt of such particulars consider all the circumstances known to him at that time and make an assessment of the delay (if any) that has been suffered by the Contractor as a result of the alleged cause and shall so notify the Contractor in writing.

(b) The Employer's Representative may in the absence of any claim make an assessment of the delay that he considers has been suffered by the Contractor as a result of any of the circumstances listed in sub-clause (1) of this Clause and shall so notify the Contractor in writing.

Interim grant of extension of time

(3)   Should the Employer's Representative consider that the delay suffered fairly entitles the Contractor to an extension of time for the substantial completion of the Works or any Section thereof such interim extension shall be granted forthwith and be notified to the Contractor in writing.

If the Contractor has made a claim for an extension of time but the Employer's Representative does not consider that the Contractor is entitled to an extension of time he shall so inform the Contractor without delay.

Assessment at due date for completion

(4)   The Employer's Representative shall not later than 14 days after the due date or extended date for completion of the Works or any Section thereof (and whether or not the Contractor has made any claim for an extension of time) consider all the circumstances known to him at that time and take action similar to that provided for in sub-clause (3) of this Clause.

Should the Employer's Representative consider the Contractor is not entitled to an extension of time he shall so notify the Employer and the Contractor.

23

...al determination of extension

(5) The Employer's Representative shall within 14 days of the issue of the Certificate of Substantial Completion for the Works or for any Section thereof review all the circumstances of the kind referred to in sub-clause (1) of this Clause and shall finally determine and certify to the Contractor with a copy to the Employer the overall extension of time (if any) to which he considers the Contractor entitled in respect of the Works or the relevant Section.

No such final review of the circumstances shall result in a decrease in any extension of time already granted by the Employer's Representative pursuant to sub-clauses (3) or (4) of this Clause.

Night and Sunday work

45 Subject to any provisions to the contrary contained in the Contract none of the Permanent and Temporary Works shall be carried out during the night or on Sundays without the permission of the Employer's Representative save when the work is unavoidable or absolutely necessary for the saving of life or property or for the safety of such Works in which case the Contractor shall immediately advise the Employer's Representative.

Provided always that this Clause shall not be applicable in the case of any work which it is customary to carry out outside normal working hours or by rotary or double shifts.

Rate of progress

46 (1) If for any reason which does not entitle the Contractor to an extension of time the rate of progress of the Works or any Section is at any time in the opinion of the Employer's Representative too slow to ensure substantial completion by the time or extended time for completion prescribed by Clauses 43 and 44 as appropriate the Employer's Representative shall notify the Contractor in writing.

The Contractor shall thereupon take such steps as are necessary and to which the Employer's Representative may consent to expedite the progress so as substantially to complete the Works or such Section by that prescribed time or extended time. The Contractor shall not be entitled to any additional payment for taking such steps.

Permission to work at night or on Sundays

(2) If as a result of any action under sub-clause (1) of this Clause the Contractor seeks the Employer's Representative's permission to do any work on Site at night or on Sundays such permission shall not be unreasonably refused.

Provision for accelerated completion

(3) If the Contractor is requested by the Employer or the Employer's Representative to complete the Works or any Section within a revised time being less than the time or extended time for completion prescribed by Clauses 43 and 44 as appropriate and the Contractor agrees so to do then any special terms and conditions of payment shall be agreed between the Contractor and the Employer before any such action is taken.

LIQUIDATED DAMAGES FOR DELAY

Liquidated damages for delay in the substantial completion of the whole of the Works

47 (1) (a) Where the whole of the Works is not divided into Sections the Appendix to the Form of Tender shall include a sum which represents the Employer's genuine pre-estimate (expressed per week or per day as the case may be) of the damages likely to be suffered by him if the whole of the Works is not substantially completed within the time prescribed by Clause 43 or any extension thereof granted under Clause 44 or by any revision thereof agreed under Clause 46(3) as the case may be.

(b) If the Contractor fails substantially to complete the whole of the Works within the time so prescribed he shall pay to the Employer the said sum for every week or day (as the case may be) which shall elapse between the date on which the prescribed time expired and the date the whole of the Works is substantially completed.

Provided that if any part of the Works is certified as substantially complete pursuant to Clause 48 before the substantial completion of the whole of the Works the said sum shall be reduced by the proportion which the value of the part so completed bears to the value of the whole of the Works.

Liquidated damages for delay in substantial completion where the whole of the Works is divided into Sections

(2) (a) Where the Works is divided into Sections (together comprising the whole of the Works) which are required to be completed within particular times as stated in the Appendix to the Form of Tender sub-clause (1) of this Clause shall not apply and the said Appendix shall include a sum in respect of each Section which represents the Employer's genuine pre-estimate (expressed per week or per day as the case may be) of the damages likely to be suffered by him if that Section is not substantially completed within the time prescribed by Clause 43 or any extension thereof granted under Clause 44 or by any revision thereof agreed under Clause 46(3) as the case may be.

(b) If the Contractor fails substantially to complete any Section within the time so prescribed he shall pay to the Employer the appropriate stated sum for every week or day (as the case may be) which shall elapse between the date on which the prescribed time expired and the date of substantial completion of that Section.

Provided that if any part of that Section is certified as substantially complete pursuant to Clause 48 before the substantial completion of the whole thereof the appropriate stated sum shall be reduced by the proportion which the value of the part bears to the value of the whole of that Section.

(c) Liquidated damages in respect of two or more Sections may where circumstances so dictate run concurrently.

Damages not a penalty

(3) All sums payable by the Contractor to the Employer pursuant to this Clause shall be paid as liquidated damages for delay and not as a penalty.

Limitation of liquidated damages

(4) (a) The total amount of liquidated damages in respect of the whole of the Works or any Section thereof shall be limited to the appropriate sum stated in the Appendix to the Form of Tender. If no such limit is stated therein then liquidated damages without limit shall apply.

(b) Should there be omitted from the Appendix to the Form of Tender any sum required to be inserted therein either by sub-clause (1)(a) or by sub-clause (2)(a) of this Clause as the case may be or if any such sum is stated to be "nil" then to that extent damages shall not be payable.

Recovery and reimbursement of liquidated damages

(5) The Employer may

(a) deduct and retain the amount of any liquidated damages becoming due under the provisions of this Clause from any sums due or which become due to the Contractor or

(b) require the Contractor to pay such amount to the Employer forthwith.

If upon a subsequent or final review of the circumstances causing delay the Employer's Representative grants a relevant extension or further extension of time the Employer shall no longer be entitled to liquidated damages in respect of the period of such extension.

Any sum in respect of such period which may already have been recovered under this Clause shall be reimbursed forthwith to the Contractor together with interest as provided in Clause 60(7) from the date on which such sums were recovered from the Contractor.

Intervention of variations etc.

(6)　If after liquidated damages have become payable in respect of any part of the Works the Employer's Representative issues a variation order under Clause 51 or adverse physical conditions or artificial obstructions within the meaning of Clause 12 are encountered or any other situation outside the Contractor's control arises any of which in the opinion of the Employer's Representative results in further delay to that part of the Works

> (a)　the Employer's Representative shall so inform the Contractor and the Employer in writing and

> (b)　the Employer's entitlement to liquidated damages in respect of that part of the Works shall be suspended until the Employer's Representative notifies the Contractor and the Employer in writing that the further delay has come to an end.

Such suspension shall not invalidate any entitlement to liquidated damages which accrued before the period of delay started to run and any monies deducted or paid in accordance with sub-clause (5) of this Clause may be retained by the Employer without incurring liability for interest thereon under Clause 60(7).

CERTIFICATE OF SUBSTANTIAL COMPLETION

Notification of substantial completion

48　(1)　When the Contractor considers that

> (a)　the whole of the Works or

> (b)　any Section in respect of which a separate time for completion is provided in the Appendix to the Form of Tender

has been substantially completed and has satisfactorily passed any final test that may be prescribed by the Contract or by Statute he may give notice in writing to that effect to the Employer's Representative. Such notice shall be accompanied by an undertaking to finish any outstanding work in accordance with the provisions of Clause 49(1).

Certificate of Substantial Completion

(2)　The Employer's Representative shall within 21 days of the date of delivery of such notice either

> (a)　issue to the Contractor (with a copy to the Employer) a Certificate of Substantial Completion stating the date on which in his opinion the Works were or the Section was substantially completed in accordance with the Contract or

> (b)　give instructions in writing to the Contractor specifying all the work which in the Employer's Representative's opinion requires to be done by the Contractor before the issue of such certificate.

If the Employer's Representative gives such instructions the Contractor shall be entitled to receive a Certificate of Substantial Completion within 21 days of completion to the satisfaction of the Employer's Representative of the work specified in the said instructions.

Operation and maintenance Instructions

(3) Prior to the issue of any Certificate of Substantial Completion under sub-clause (2) of this Clause the Contractor shall provide the Employer with operation and maintenance instructions in sufficient detail to enable the Works or Section being taken over by the Employer to be operated maintained dismantled re-assembled and adjusted satisfactorily.

Premature use by Employer

(4) If any substantial part of the Works has been occupied or used by the Employer other than as provided in the Contract the Contractor may request in writing and the Employer's Representative shall issue a Certificate of Substantial Completion in respect thereof. Such certificate shall take effect from the date of delivery of the Contractor's request and upon the issue of such certificate the Contractor shall be deemed to have undertaken to complete any outstanding work in that part of the Works during the Defects Correction Period.

Substantial completion of other parts of the Works

(5) If the Employer's Representative considers that any part of the Works has been substantially completed and has passed any final test that may be prescribed by the Contract he may issue a Certificate of Substantial Completion in respect of that part of the Works before completion of the whole of the Works and upon the issue of such certificate the Contractor shall be deemed to have undertaken to complete any outstanding work in that part of the Works during the Defects Correction Period.

Reinstatement of ground

(6) A Certificate of Substantial Completion given in respect of any Section or part of the Works before substantial completion of the whole shall not be deemed to certify completion of any ground or surfaces requiring reinstatement unless such certificate shall expressly so state.

OUTSTANDING WORK AND DEFECTS

Work outstanding 49

(1) The undertaking to be given under Clause 48(1) may by agreement between the Employer's Representative and the Contractor specify a time or times within which the outstanding work shall be completed. If no such times are specified any outstanding work shall be completed as soon as practicable during the Defects Correction Period.

Carrying out of work of repair etc.

(2) The Contractor shall deliver up to the Employer the Works and each Section and part thereof at or as soon as practicable after the end of the relevant Defects Correction Period in the condition required by the Contract (fair wear and tear excepted) to the satisfaction of the Employer's Representative.

To this end the Contractor shall repair amend reconstruct rectify and make good defects of whatever nature notified to him in writing by the Employer's Representative during the relevant Defects Correction Period or within 14 days after its expiry as a result of an inspection made by or on behalf of the Employer's Representative prior to its expiry.

Cost of work of repair etc.

(3) All work required under sub-clause (2) of this Clause shall be carried out by the Contractor at his own expense if in the Employer's Representative's opinion it is necessary due to failure by the Contractor to comply with any of his obligations under the Contract. In any other event the value of such work shall be ascertained and paid for as if it were additional work.

Remedy on Contractor's failure to carry out work required

(4) If the Contractor fails to do any such work as aforesaid the Employer shall be entitled to carry out that work by his own workpeople or by other contractors and if it is work which the Contractor should have carried out at his own expense the Employer shall be entitled to recover

the cost thereof from the Contractor and may deduct the same from any monies that are or may become due to the Contractor.

Contractor to search 50 The Contractor shall if required by the Employer's Representative in writing carry out such searches tests or trials as may be necessary to determine the cause of any defect imperfection or fault.

Unless the defect imperfection or fault is one for which the Contractor is liable under the Contract the cost of the work carried out by the Contractor as aforesaid shall be borne by the Employer. If the defect imperfection or fault is one for which the Contractor is liable the cost of the work carried out as aforesaid shall be borne by the Contractor and he shall in such case repair rectify and make good the defect imperfection or fault at his own expense in accordance with Clause 49.

ALTERATIONS AND ADDITIONAL PAYMENTS

Ordered variations to Employer's Requirements 51 (1) The Employer's Representative shall have power after consultation with the Contractor's Representative to vary the Employer's Requirements. Such variations may include additions and/or omissions and may be ordered at any time up to the end of the Defects Correction Period for the whole of the Works.

Ordered variations to be in writing (2) All variations shall be ordered in writing but the provisions of Clause 2(5) in respect of oral instructions shall apply.

Variation not to affect Contract (3) No variation ordered under this Clause shall in any way vitiate or invalidate the Contract but the fair and reasonable value (if any) of all such variations shall be taken into account in ascertaining the amount of the Contract Price except to the extent that such variation is necessitated by the Contractor's default.

Valuation of ordered variations 52 (1) When requested by the Employer's Representative the Contractor shall submit his quotation for the work as varied and his estimate of any delay. Wherever possible the value and delay consequences (if any) of each variation shall be agreed before the order is issued or before work starts.

(2) In all other cases the valuation of variations ordered by the Employer's Representative in accordance with Clause 51 shall be ascertained as follows.

(a) As soon as possible after receipt of the variation order the Contractor shall submit to the Employer's Representative

(i) his quotation for any extra or substituted works necessitated by the variation having due regard to any rates or prices included in the Contract and

(ii) his estimate of any delay occasioned thereby and

(iii) his estimate of the cost of any such delay.

(b) Within 14 days of receiving the said submissions the Employer's Representative shall

(i) accept the same or

(ii) negotiate with the Contractor thereon.

(c) Upon reaching agreement with the Contractor the Contract Price shall be amended accordingly.

(d) In the absence of agreement the Employer's Representative shall notify the Contractor of what in his opinion is a fair and reasonable valuation and thereafter shall make such interim valuations for the purposes of Clause 60 as may be appropriate.

Daywork (3) The Employer's Representative may if in his opinion it is necessary or desirable order in writing that any additional or substituted work shall be executed on a daywork basis in accordance with the provisions of Clause 56(3).

Additional payments 53 (1) If the Contractor intends to claim any additional payment pursuant to any Clause of these Conditions other than Clause 52(1) he shall give notice in writing of his intention to the Employer's Representative as soon as may be reasonable and in any event within 28 days after the happening of the events giving rise to the claim.

Upon the happening of such events the Contractor shall keep such contemporary records as may reasonably be necessary to support any claim he may subsequently wish to make.

(2) Without necessarily admitting the Employer's liability the Employer's Representative may upon receipt of a notice under this Clause instruct the Contractor to keep such contemporary records or further contemporary records as the case may be as are reasonable and may be material to the claim of which notice has been given and the Contractor shall keep such records.

The Contractor shall permit the Employer's Representative to inspect all records kept pursuant to this Clause and shall supply him with copies thereof as and when the Employer's Representative shall so instruct.

(3) After the giving of a notice to the Employer's Representative under this Clause the Contractor shall as soon as is reasonable in all the circumstances send to the Employer's Representative a first interim account giving full and detailed particulars of the amount claimed to that date and of the grounds upon which the claim is based.

Thereafter at such intervals as the Employer's Representative may reasonably require the Contractor shall send to the Employer's Representative further up to date accounts giving the accumulated total of the claim and any further grounds upon which it is based.

(4) If the Contractor fails to comply with any of the provisions of this Clause in respect of any claim which he shall seek to make then the Contractor shall be entitled to payment in respect thereof only to the extent that the Employer's Representative has not been prevented from or substantially prejudiced by such failure in investigating the said claim.

(5) The Contractor shall be entitled to have included in any interim payment certified by the Employer's Representative pursuant to Clause 60 such amount in respect of any claim as the Employer's Representative may consider due to the Contractor provided that the Contractor shall have supplied sufficient particulars to enable the Employer's Representative to determine the amount due.

If such particulars are insufficient to substantiate the whole of the claim the Contractor shall be entitled to payment in respect of such part of the claim as the particulars may substantiate to the satisfaction of the Employer's Representative.

MATERIALS AND CONTRACTOR'S EQUIPMENT

Non-removal of materials and Contractor's Equipment

54 (1) No Contractor's Equipment Temporary Works materials for Temporary Works or other goods or materials owned by the Contractor and brought on to the Site for the purposes of the Contract shall be removed without the written consent of the Employer's Representative which consent shall not unreasonably be withheld where the items in question are no longer immediately required for the purposes of the completion of the Works.

Vesting of goods and materials not on Site

(2) With a view to securing payment under Clause 60(1)(c) the Contractor may (and shall if the Employer's Representative so directs) transfer to the Employer the property in goods and materials listed in the Appendix to the Form of Tender or as subsequently agreed between the Contractor and the Employer before the same are delivered to the Site provided that the goods and materials

(a) have been manufactured or prepared and are substantially ready for incorporation in the Works and

(b) are the property of the Contractor or the contract for the supply of the same expressly provides that the property therein shall pass unconditionally to the Contractor upon the Contractor taking the action referred to in sub-clause (3) of this Clause.

Action by Contractor

(3) The intention of the Contractor to transfer the property in any goods or materials to the Employer in accordance with this Clause shall be evidenced by the Contractor taking or causing the supplier of those goods or materials to take the following actions.

(a) Provide to the Employer's Representative documentary evidence that the property of the said goods or materials has vested in the Contractor.

(b) Suitably mark or otherwise plainly identify the goods and materials so as to show that their destination is the Site that they are the property of the Employer and (where they are not stored at the premises of the Contractor) to whose order they are held.

(c) Set aside and store the said goods and materials so marked and identified to the satisfaction of the Employer's Representative.

(d) Send to the Employer's Representative a schedule listing and giving the value of every item of the goods and materials so set aside and stored and inviting him to inspect them.

Vesting in the Employer

(4) Upon the Employer's Representative approving in writing the transfer in ownership of any goods and materials for the purposes of this Clause they shall vest in and become the absolute property of the Employer and thereafter shall be in the possession of the Contractor for the sole purpose of delivering them to the Employer and incorporating them in the Works and shall not be within the ownership control or disposition of the Contractor. Provided always that

(a) approval by the Employer's Representative for the purposes of this Clause or any payment certified by him in respect of goods and materials pursuant to Clause 60 shall be without prejudice to the exercise of any power of the Employer's Representative contained in this Contract to reject any goods or materials which are not in accordance with the provisions of the Contract and upon any such rejection the property in the rejected goods or materials shall immediately re-vest in the Contractor and

(b) the Contractor shall be responsible for any loss or damage to such goods or materials and for the cost of storing handling and transporting the same and shall effect such additional insurance as may be necessary to cover the risk of such loss or damage from any cause.

Lien on goods and materials (5) Neither the Contractor nor a sub-contractor nor any other person shall have a lien on any goods or materials which have vested in the Employer under sub-clause (4) of this Clause for any sum due to the Contractor sub-contractor or other person and the Contractor shall take all steps reasonably necessary to ensure that the title of the Employer and the exclusion of any such lien are brought to the notice of sub-contractors and other persons dealing with such goods or materials.

Delivery to the Employer of vested goods or materials (6) Upon cessation of the employment of the Contractor under this Contract before the completion of the Works whether as a result of the operation of Clause 63 64 or 65 or otherwise the Contractor shall deliver to the Employer any goods or materials the property in which has vested in the Employer by virtue of sub-clause (4) of this Clause and if he fails to do so the Employer may enter any premises of the Contractor or of any sub-contractor and remove such goods and materials and recover the cost of doing so from the Contractor.

Incorporation in sub-contracts (7) The Contractor shall incorporate provisions equivalent to those provided in this Clause in every sub-contract in which provision is to be made for the payment in respect of goods or materials before the same have been delivered to the Site.

MEASUREMENT

Quantities 55 (1) Where the Contract includes any bill of quantities schedule of works or Contingencies the quantities set out therein shall be deemed to be the estimated quantities of the work but they are not to be taken as the actual or correct quantities of work to be constructed by the Contractor in fulfilment of his obligations under the Contract.

(2) No error in description in or omission from any such bill of quantities schedule of works or Contingency or in any schedule of rates shall vitiate the Contract nor release the Contractor from any of his obligations or liabilities thereunder.

Attending for measurement 56 (1) If and to the extent that it becomes necessary to measure any part of the Works either the Contractor's or the Employer's Representative shall give reasonable notice in writing to the other requiring him to attend or send a qualified agent to assist in making such measurement.

(2) Should either the Contractor's or the Employer's Representative not attend or neglect or omit to send such agent when so requested then the measurement made by the other or approved by him shall be taken to be the correct measurement of the work.

Daywork (3) Where any work is carried out on a daywork basis the Contractor shall be paid for such work under the conditions and at the rates and prices set out in the daywork schedule included in the Contract or failing the inclusion of a daywork schedule he shall be paid at the rates and prices and under the conditions contained in the "Schedule of Dayworks carried out incidental to Contract Work" issued by the Federation of Civil Engineering Contractors current at the date of the execution of the daywork.

The Contractor shall furnish to the Employer's Representative such records receipts and other documentation as may be necessary to prove amounts paid and/or costs incurred. Such returns shall be in the form and delivered at the times the Employer's Representative shall direct and shall be agreed within a reasonable time.

Before ordering materials the Contractor shall if so required submit to the Employer's Representative quotations for the same for his approval.

57 Not used.

PRIME COST ITEMS

Use of Contingency and Prime Cost Items **58** (1)   The Contractor shall not commence work on any Contingency or Prime Cost Item until he has secured the consent thereto of the Employer's Representative which consent shall not unreasonably be withheld.

Valuation and payment (2)   Contingencies and Prime Cost Items shall be valued and paid for in accordance with Clause 52 or as the Contract otherwise provides. The percentage to be used for overheads and profit in adjusting the Prime Cost element of any such item shall be the figure stated therefor in the Appendix to the Form of Tender.

59 Not used.

CERTIFICATES AND PAYMENT

Interim statements **60** (1)   The Contractor shall submit to the Employer's Representative at such times and in such form as the Contract prescribes statements showing

(a)   the amounts which in the Contractor's opinion are due under the Contract

and where appropriate showing separately

(b)   each amount expended against Contingencies and Prime Cost Items

(c)   a list of any goods or materials delivered to the Site for but not yet incorporated in the Permanent Works and their value

(d)   a list of any goods or materials which have not yet been delivered to the Site but of which the property has vested in the Employer pursuant to Clause 54 and their value and

(e)   the estimated amounts to which the Contractor considers himself entitled in connection with all other matters for which provision is made under the Contract

unless in the opinion of the Contractor such values and amounts together will not justify the issue of an interim certificate.

Interim payments (2)   Within 28 days of the date of delivery of the Contractor's statement to the Employer's Representative in accordance with sub-clause (1) of this Clause the Employer's Representative shall either

(a)   where a payment schedule is included in the Contract certify

(i)   when the progress of the Works or any part thereof has reached the state required for the payment of the relevant interim or stage payment and

(ii)   the amount of such payment less a retention as provided in sub-clause (5) of this Clause or

(b)   where no such schedule is included in the Contract certify

(i) the amount which in the opinion of the Employer's Representative on the basis of the Contractor's statement is due to the Contractor other than on account of sub-clauses (1)(c) and (1)(d) of this Clause less a retention as provided in sub-clause (5) of this Clause and

(ii) such amounts (if any) as the Employer's Representative may consider proper (but in no case exceeding the percentage of the value stated in the Appendix to the Form of Tender) in respect of sub-clauses (1)(c) and (1)(d) of this Clause

and the Employer shall pay to the Contractor such amounts as become due thereby after deducting any previous payments on account.

Minimum amount of certificate

(3) Until the whole of the Works has been certified as substantially complete in accordance with Clause 48 the Employer's Representative shall not be bound to issue an interim certificate for a sum less than that stated in the Appendix to the Form of Tender but thereafter he shall be bound to do so and the certification and payment of amounts due to the Contractor shall be in accordance with the time limits contained in this Clause.

Final account

(4) Not later than 3 months after the date of the Defects Correction Certificate the Contractor shall submit to the Employer's Representative a statement of the final account and supporting documentation showing in detail the value in accordance with the Contract of the Works carried out together with all further sums which the Contractor considers to be due to him under the Contract up to the date of the Defects Correction Certificate.

Within 3 months after receipt of this final account and of all information reasonably required for its verification the Employer's Representative shall issue a certificate stating the amount which in his opinion is finally due under the Contract from the Employer to the Contractor or from the Contractor to the Employer (as the case may be) up to the date of the Defects Correction Certificate and after giving credit to the Employer for all amounts previously paid by the Employer and for all sums to which the Employer is entitled under the Contract.

Such amount shall subject to Clause 47 be paid to or by the Contractor as the case may require within 28 days of the date of the certificate.

Retention

(5) The retention to be made pursuant to sub-clause (2) of this Clause shall be the difference between

(a) an amount calculated at the rate indicated in and up to the limit set out in the Appendix to the Form of Tender upon the amount due to the Contractor other than any amount due under sub-clause 2(b)(ii) of this Clause and

(b) any payment which shall have become due under sub-clause (6) of this Clause.

Payment of retention

(6) (a) Upon the issue of a Certificate of Substantial Completion in respect of any Section or part of the Works there shall become due to the Contractor one half of such proportion of the retention money deductible to date under sub-clause (5)(a) of this Clause as the value of the Section or part bears to the value of the whole of the Works completed to date as certified under sub-clause (2) of this Clause and such amount shall be added to the amount next certified as due to the Contractor under sub-clause (2) of this Clause.

The total of the amounts released shall in no event exceed one half of the limit of retention set out in the Appendix to the Form of Tender.

(b) Upon issue of the Certificate of Substantial Completion in respect of the whole of the Works there shall become due to the Contractor one half of the retention money calculated in accordance with sub-clause (5)(a) of this Clause. The amount so due (or the balance thereof over and above such payments already made pursuant to sub-clause (6)(a) of this Clause) shall be paid within 14 days of the issue of the said certificate.

(c) At the end of the Defects Correction Period or if more than one the last of such periods the remainder of the retention money shall be paid to the Contractor within 14 days notwithstanding that at that time there may be outstanding claims by the Contractor against the Employer.

Provided that if at that time there remains to be carried out by the Contractor any outstanding work referred to under Clause 48 or any work ordered pursuant to Clauses 49 or 50 the Employer may withhold payment until the completion of such work of so much of the said remainder as shall in the opinion of the Employer's Representative represent the cost of the work remaining to be executed.

Interest on overdue payments

(7) In the event of

(a) failure by the Employer's Representative to certify or the Employer to make payment in accordance with sub-clauses (2) (4) or (6) of this Clause or

(b) any finding of an arbitrator to such effect

the Employer shall pay to the Contractor interest compounded monthly for each day on which any payment is overdue or which should have been certified and paid at a rate equivalent to 2% per annum above the base lending rate of the bank specified in the Appendix to the Form of Tender.

If in an arbitration pursuant to Clause 66 the arbitrator holds that any sum or additional sum should have been certified by a particular date in accordance with the aforementioned sub-clauses but was not so certified this shall be regarded for the purposes of this sub-clause as a failure to certify such sum or additional sum. Such sum or additional sum shall be regarded as overdue for payment 28 days after the date by which the arbitrator holds that the Employer's Representative should have certified the sum or if no such date is identified by the arbitrator shall be regarded as overdue for payment from the date of the Certificate of Substantial Completion for the whole of the Works.

Correction and withholding of certificates

(8) The Employer's Representative shall have power to omit from any certificate the value of any work done goods or materials supplied or services rendered with which he may for the time being be dissatisfied and for that purpose or for any other reason which to him may seem proper may by any certificate delete correct or modify any sum or statement of fact previously certified by him.

Copy of certificate for Contractor

(9) Every certificate issued by the Employer's Representative pursuant to this Clause shall be sent to the Employer and at the same time copied to the Contractor with such detailed explanation as may be necessary.

Payment advice

(10) Where a payment made in accordance with this Clause differs in any respect from the amount certified by the Employer's Representative the Employer shall notify the Contractor forthwith with full details showing how the amount being paid has been calculated.

Defects Correction Certificate

61 (1) At the end of the Defects Correction Period or where there is more than one such period at the end of the last of such periods and when all outstanding work referred to under Clause 48 and all work of repair amendment reconstruction rectification and making good of defects imperfections shrinkages and other faults referred to under Clauses 49 and 50 has been completed the Employer's Representative shall issue to the Employer (with a copy to the Contractor) a Defects Correction Certificate stating the date on which the Contractor has completed his obligations to construct and complete the Works to the Employer's Representative's satisfaction.

Unfulfilled obligations

(2) The issue of the Defects Correction Certificate shall not be taken as relieving either the Contractor or the Employer from any liability the one towards the other arising out of or in any way connected with the performance of their respective obligations under the Contract.

Manuals and drawings

(3) Prior to the issue of the Defects Correction Certificate the Contractor shall

(a) submit to the Employer's Representative for his approval one set of draft operation and maintenance manuals together with as-constructed record drawings in sufficient detail to enable the Employer to operate maintain dismantle reassemble and adjust the Permanent Works and

(b) once the Employer's Representative has given approval thereto supply to the Employer three sets of the finally approved manuals and drawings.

REMEDIES AND POWERS

Urgent repairs 62 If in the opinion of the Employer's Representative any remedial or other work or repair is urgently necessary by reason of any accident or failure or other event occurring to in or in connection with the Works or any part thereof either during the carrying out of the Works or during the Defects Correction Period the Employer's Representative shall so inform the Contractor with confirmation in writing.

Thereafter if the Contractor is unable or unwilling to carry out such work or repair at once the Employer may himself carry out the said work or repair using his own or other workpeople.

If the work or repair so carried out by the Employer is work which in the opinion of the Employer's Representative the Contractor was liable to carry out at his own expense under the Contract all costs and charges properly incurred by the Employer in so doing shall on demand be paid by the Contractor to the Employer or may be deducted by the Employer from any monies due or which may become due to the Contractor.

Frustration 63 (1) If any circumstance outside the control of both parties arises during the currency of the Contract which renders it impossible or illegal for either party to fulfil his contractual obligations the Works shall be deemed to be abandoned upon the service by one party upon the other of written notice to that effect.

War clause

(2) If during the currency of the Contract there is an outbreak of war (whether war is declared or not) in which Great Britain is engaged on a scale involving general mobilization of the armed forces of the Crown

(a) the Contractor shall for a period of 28 days reckoned from midnight on the date that the order for general mobilization is given continue so far as is physically possible to execute the Works in accordance with the Contract and

(b) if substantial completion of the whole of the Works is not achieved before the said period of 28 days has expired the Works shall thereupon be deemed to be abandoned unless the parties otherwise agree.

Removal of Contractor's equipment

(3) Upon abandonment of the Works pursuant to sub-clauses (1) or (2)(b) of this Clause the Contractor shall with all reasonable dispatch remove from the Site all Contractor's Equipment.

In the event of any failure so to do the Employer shall have like powers to those contained in Clause 33(2) to dispose of any Contractor's Equipment.

Payment on abandonment

(4) Upon abandonment of the Works pursuant to sub-clauses (1) or (2)(b) of this Clause the Employer shall pay the Contractor (in so far as such amounts or items have not already been covered by payments on account made to the Contractor) the Contract value of all work carried out prior to the date of abandonment and in addition

(a) the amounts payable in respect of any preliminary items so far as the work or service comprised therein has been carried out or performed and a proper proportion of any such items which have been partially carried out or performed

(b) the cost of materials or goods reasonably ordered for the Works which have been delivered to the Contractor or of which the Contractor is legally liable to accept delivery (such materials or goods becoming the property of the Employer upon such payment being made to the Contractor)

(c) a sum being the amount of any expenditure reasonably incurred by the Contractor in the expectation of completing the whole of the Works insofar as such expenditure has not been recovered by any other payments referred to in this sub-clause and

(d) the reasonable cost of removal under sub-clause (3) of this Clause.

To this end and without prejudice to the provisions of sub-clause (5) of this Clause the provisions of Clause 60(4) shall apply to this sub-clause as if the date of abandonment was the date of issue of the Defects Correction Certificate.

Works substantially completed

(5) If upon abandonment of the Works any Section or part of the Works has been substantially completed in accordance with Clause 48 or is completed so far as to be useable then in connection therewith

(a) the Contractor may at his discretion and in lieu of his obligations under Clauses 49 and 50 allow against the sum due to him pursuant to sub-clause (4) of this Clause the cost (calculated as at the date of abandonment) of repair rectification and making good for which he would have been liable under the said Clauses had they continued to be applicable and

(b) the Employer shall not be entitled to withhold payment under Clause 60(6)(c) of the second half of the retention money or any part thereof except such sum as the Contractor may allow under the provisions of the last preceding paragraph.

Contract to continue in force

(6) Save as aforesaid the Contract shall continue to have full force and effect.

Failure to pay the Contractor 64

(1) In the event of failure by the Employer's Representative to certify or the Employer to pay the Contractor the amount due (subject to any

deduction that the Employer is entitled to make under the Contract) in accordance with Clause 60 within 21 days after the expiry of the time therein stated then the Contractor may after giving 7 days notice in writing to the Employer (with a copy to the Employer's Representative) suspend work or reduce the rate of work.

Resumption of work

(2) Upon payment by the Employer of the amount due (including interest pursuant to Clause 60(7)) the Contractor shall resume normal working as soon as is reasonably possible.

Delay and extra cost

(3) If the Contractor suffers delay and/or incurs additional cost as a result of suspending or reducing the rate of work under sub-clause (1) of this Clause the Employer's Representative shall determine

(a) any extension of time to which the Contractor is entitled under Clause 44 and

(b) subject to Clause 53 the amount of such additional cost.

Default of Employer

(4) In the event of

(a) failure by the Employer's Representative to certify or the Employer to pay the Contractor the amount due (subject to any deduction that the Employer is entitled to make under the Contract) in accordance with Clause 60 within 56 days after the expiry of the time therein stated

or if the Employer

(b) assigns or attempts to assign the Contract or any part thereof or any benefit or interest thereunder without the prior written consent of the Contractor or

(c) (i) becomes bankrupt or presents his petition in bankruptcy or

(ii) has a receiving order or administration order made against him or

(iii) makes an arrangement with or an assignment in favour of his creditors or

(iv) agrees to perform the Contract under a committee of inspection of his creditors or

(v) (being a corporation) appoints a receiver or administrator or goes into liquidation (other than a voluntary liquidation for the purposes of amalgamation or reconstruction) or

(d) has an execution levied on his goods which is not stayed or discharged within 28 days

then the Contractor may after giving 7 days notice in writing to the Employer specifying the default terminate his employment under the Contract without thereby avoiding the Contract or releasing the Employer from any of his obligations or liabilities under the Contract.

Provided that the Contractor may extend the period of notice to give the Employer an opportunity to remedy his default.

Removal of Contractor's Equipment

(5) Upon expiry of the 7 days notice referred to in sub-clause (4) of this Clause and notwithstanding the provisions of Clause 54 the Contractor shall with all reasonable despatch remove from the site all Contractor's Equipment.

Payment upon termination

(6) Upon termination of the Contractor's employment pursuant to sub-clause (4) of this Clause the Employer shall be under the same obligations with regard to payment as if the Works had been abandoned under the provisions of Clause 63.

Provided that in addition to payments specified under Clause 63(4) the Employer shall pay to the Contractor

(a) any amount to which the Contractor is entitled under sub-clause (3) of this Clause and

(b) the amount of any loss or damage to the Contractor arising from or as a consequence of such termination.

Default of Contractor

65 (1) If the Contractor

(a) assigns or attempts to assign the Contract or any part thereof or any benefit or interest thereunder without the prior written consent of the Employer or

(b) is in breach of Clause 4(1) or

(c) (i) becomes bankrupt or presents his petition in bankruptcy or

(ii) has a receiving order or administration order made against him or

(iii) makes an arrangement with or an assignment in favour of his creditors or

(iv) agrees to carry out the Contract under a committee of inspection of his creditors or

(v) (being a corporation) appoints a receiver or administrator or goes into liquidation (other than a voluntary liquidation for the purposes of amalgamation or reconstruction) or

(d) has an execution levied on his goods which is not stayed or discharged within 28 days

or if the Employer's Representative certifies in writing to the Employer with a copy to the Contractor that in his opinion the Contractor

(e) has abandoned the Contract without due cause or

(f) without reasonable excuse has failed to commence the Works in accordance with Clause 41 or

(g) has suspended the progress of the Works without due cause for 14 days after receiving from the Employer's Representative written notice to proceed or

(h) has failed to remove goods or materials from the Site or to pull down and replace work for 14 days after receiving from the Employer's Representative written notice that the said goods materials or work has been condemned and rejected by the Employer's Representative or

(j) despite previous warnings by the Employer's Representative in writing is failing to proceed with the Works with due diligence or is otherwise persistently or fundamentally in breach of his obligations under the Contract

then the Employer may after giving 7 days notice in writing to the Contractor specifying the default enter upon the Works and any other parts of the Site provided by the Employer and expel the Contractor therefrom without thereby avoiding the Contract or releasing the Contractor from any of his obligations or liabilites under the Contract.

Where a notice of termination is given pursuant to a certificate issued by the Employer's Representative under this sub-clause it shall be given as soon as is reasonably possible after receipt of the certificate.

Provided that the Employer may extend the period of notice to give the Contractor an opportunity to remedy the default.

Completing the Works

(2)   Where the Employer has entered upon the Works and any other parts of the Site as set out in sub-clause (1) of this Clause he may

(a)   complete the Works himself or

(b)   employ any other contractor to complete the Works

and in either case may use for such completion any of the Contractor's Equipment Temporary Works goods and materials on any part of the Site and/or those which have been deemed to become the property of the Employer under Clause 54.

The Employer may at any time sell any of the said Contractor's Equipment Temporary Works and unused goods and materials and apply the proceeds of sale in or towards the satisfaction of any sums due or which may become due to him from the Contractor under the Contract.

Assignment to Employer

(3)   Where the Employer has entered upon the Works and any other parts of the Site as hereinbefore provided the Contractor shall if so instructed by the Employer's Representative in writing within 7 days of such entry assign to the Employer the benefit of any agreement which the Contractor may have entered into for the supply of any goods or materials and/or for the carrying out of any work for the purposes of the Contract.

Valuation at date of termination

(4)   As soon as may be practicable after any such entry and expulsion by the Employer the Employer's Representative shall fix and determine as at the time of such entry and expulsion

(a)   the amount (if any) which has been reasonably earned by or would reasonably accrue to the Contractor in respect of work actually done by him under the Contract and

(b)   the value of any unused or partially used goods and materials and any Contractor's Equipment and Temporary Works which had been deemed to become the property of the Employer under Clause 54

and shall certify accordingly.

The said determination may be carried out *ex parte* or by or after reference to the parties or after such investigation or enquiry as the Employer's Representative may think fit to make or institute.

Payment after termination

(5)   If the Employer enters and expels the Contractor under this Clause he shall not be liable to pay to the Contractor any money on account of the Contract until the end of the Defects Correction Period and thereafter until the costs of completion damages for delay in completion (if any) and all other expenses incurred by the Employer have been ascertained and the amount thereof certified by the Employer's Representative.

The Contractor shall then be entitled to receive only such sum or sums (if any) as the Employer's Representative may certify would have been due to him upon due completion by him after deducting the said amount. But if such amount shall exceed the sum which would have been payable to the Contractor on due completion by him then the Contractor shall upon demand pay to the Employer the amount of such excess and it shall be deemed a debt due by the Contractor to the Employer and shall be recoverable accordingly.

SETTLEMENT OF DISPUTES

Settlement of disputes   **66**   (1)   Except as otherwise provided in these Conditions if a dispute of any kind whatsoever arises between the Employer and the Contractor in connection with or arising out of the Contract or the carrying out of the Works including any dispute as to any decision opinion instruction direction certificate or valuation of the Employer's Representative (whether during the progress of the Works or after their completion and whether before or after the determination abandonment or breach of the Contract) it shall be settled in accordance with the following provisions.

Notice of Dispute   (2)   For the purpose of sub-clauses (2) to (5) inclusive of this Clause a dispute shall be deemed to arise when one party serves on the other a notice in writing (herinafter called the Notice of Dispute) stating the nature of the dispute. Provided that no Notice of Dispute may be served unless the party wishing to do so has first taken any steps or invoked any procedure available elsewhere in the Contract in connection with the subject matter of such dispute and the other party or the Employer's Representative as the case may be has

     (a)   taken such step as may be required or

     (b)   been allowed a reasonable time to take any such action.

Conciliation   (3)   Every dispute notified under sub-clause (2) of this Clause if not already settled shall after the period of one calendar month from service of the Notice of Dispute be referred to conciliation in accordance with the Institution of Civil Engineers' Conciliation Procedure (1988) or any modification thereof being in force at the date of such referral. The conciliator shall make his recommendation in writing and give notice of the same to the Employer and the Contractor within three calendar months of the service of the Notice of Dispute.

Effect on Contractor and Employer   (4)   Unless the Contract has already been determined or abandoned the Contractor shall in every case continue to proceed with the Works with all due diligence.

The Contractor and the Employer shall both give effect forthwith to every recommendation of the conciliator. Such recommendations shall be final and binding upon the Contractor and the Employer unless and until the recommendation of the conciliator is revised by an arbitrator as hereinafter provided and an award made and published.

Arbitration   (5)   Where either

     (a) the Employer or the Contractor is dissatisfied with any recommendation of a conciliator appointed under sub-clause (3) of this Clause or

     (b) the conciliator fails to give such recommendation for a period of three calendar months after the service of the Notice of Dispute

then either the Employer or the Contractor may within three calendar months after receiving notice of the conciliator's recommendation or within three calendar months after the expiry of the period of three months referred to in paragraph (b) of this sub-clause (as the case may be) refer the dispute to the arbitration of a person to be agreed upon by the parties by serving on the other party a written Notice to Refer.

President or Vice-President to act

(6) (a) If the parties fail to appoint an arbitrator within one calendar month of either party serving on the other party written Notice to Concur in the appointment of an arbitrator the dispute shall be referred to a person to be appointed on the application of either party by the President for the time being of the Institution of Civil Engineers.

(b) If an arbitrator declines the appointment or after appointment is removed by order of a competent court or is incapable of acting or dies and the parties do not within one calendar month of the vacancy arising fill the vacancy then either party may apply to the President for the time being of the Institution of Civil Engineers to appoint another arbitrator to fill the vacancy.

(c) In any case where the President for the time being of the Institution of Civil Engineers is not able to exercise the functions conferred on him by this Clause the said functions shall be exercised on his behalf by a Vice-President for the time being of the said Institution.

Arbitration – procedure and powers

(7) (a) Any reference to arbitration under this Clause shall be deemed to be a submission to arbitration within the meaning of the Arbitration Acts 1950 to 1979 or any statutory re-enactment or amendment thereof for the time being in force. The reference shall be conducted in accordance with the Institution of Civil Engineers Arbitration Procedure (1983) or any amendment or modification thereof being in force at the time of the appointment of the arbitrator. Such arbitrator shall have full power to open up review and revise any decision opinion instruction direction certificate or valuation of the Employer's Representative.

(b) Neither party shall be limited in the proceedings before such arbitrator to the evidence or arguments put before the conciliator for the purpose of obtaining his recommendation under sub-clause (3) of this Clause.

(c) The award of the arbitrator shall be binding on all parties.

(d) Unless the parties otherwise agree in writing any reference to arbitration may proceed notwithstanding that the Works are not then complete or alleged to be complete.

Witnesses

(8) (a) No decision opinion instruction direction certificate or valuation given by the Employer's Representative shall disqualify him from being called as a witness and giving evidence before the conciliator or arbitrator on any matter whatsoever relevant to the dispute.

(b) All matters and information placed before the conciliator pursuant to a reference under sub-clause (3) of this Clause shall be deemed to be submitted to him without prejudice and the conciliator shall not be called as witness by the parties or anyone claiming through them in connection with any arbitration or other legal proceedings arising out of or connected with any matter so referred to him.

APPLICATION TO SCOTLAND ETC.

Application to Scotland

67 (1) If the Works are situated in Scotland the Contract shall in all respects be construed and operate as a Scottish contract and shall be interpreted in accordance with Scots law and the provisions of sub-clause (2) of this Clause shall apply.

(2)   In the application of these Conditions and in particular Clause 66 thereof

   (a)   the word "arbiter" shall be substituted for the word "arbitrator"

   (b)   for any reference to the "Arbitration Acts" there shall be substituted reference to the "Arbitration (Scotland) Act 1894"

   (c)   for any reference to the Institution of Civil Engineers Arbitration Procedure (1983) there shall be substituted a reference to the Institution of Civil Engineers Arbitration Procedure (Scotland) (1983) and

   (d)   notwithstanding any of the other provisions of these Conditions nothing therein shall be construed as excluding or otherwise affecting the right of a party to arbitration to call in terms of Section 3 of the Administration of Justice (Scotland) Act 1972 for the arbiter to state a case.

Application to Northern Ireland

(3)   If the Works are situated in Northern Ireland the Contract shall in all respects be construed and operate as a Northern Irish contract and shall be interpreted in accordance with the law of Northern Ireland and the provisions of sub-clause (4) of this Clause shall apply.

(4)   In the application of these Conditions and in particular Clause 66 thereof for any reference to the "Arbitration Acts" there shall be substituted reference to the "Arbitration (Northern Ireland) Act 1937".

Application elsewhere

(5)   If the Works are situated in a country or jurisdiction other than England and Wales Scotland or Northern Ireland the Contract and the provisions for disputes settlement shall in all respects be construed and operate and be interpreted in accordance with the law of that country or jurisdiction.

NOTICES

Service of notices on Contractor   68

(1) Any notice to be given to the Contractor under the terms of the Contract shall be served in writing at the Contractor's principal place of business (or in the event of the Contractor being a Company to or at its registered office).

Service of notices on Employer

(2)   Any notice to be given to the Employer under the terms of the Contract shall be served in writing at the Employer's last known address (or in the event of the Employer being a Company to or at its registered office).

TAX MATTERS

Labour-tax fluctuations   69

(1)   The rates and prices contained in the Contract shall be deemed to take account of the levels and incidence at the date for return of tenders of the taxes levies contributions premiums or refunds (including national insurance contributions but excluding income tax and any levy payable under the Industrial Training Act 1964) which are by law payable by or to the Contractor and his sub-contractors in respect of their employees engaged on the Contract.

The rates and prices contained in the Contract do not take account of any level or incidence of the aforesaid matters where at the date for return of tenders such level or incidence does not then have effect but although then known is to take effect at some later date.

(2)   If after the date for return of tenders there shall occur any change in the level and/or incidence of any such taxes levies contributions premiums or refunds the Contractor shall so inform the Employer's Representative and the net increase or decrease shall be taken into account in arriving at the Contract Price. The Contractor shall supply the information necessary to support any consequent adjustment to the Contract Price.

All certificates for payment issued after submission of such information shall take due account of the additions or deductions to which such information relates.

Value Added Tax **70** (1)   The Contractor shall be deemed not to have allowed in his tender for the tax payable by him as a taxable person to the Commissioners of Customs and Excise being tax chargeable on any taxable supplies to the Employer which are to be made under the Contract.

Employer's Representative's certificates net of Value Added Tax (2)   All certificates issued by the Employer's Representative under Clause 60 shall be net of Value Added Tax.

In addition to the payments due under such certificates the Employer shall separately identify and pay to the Contractor any Value Added Tax properly chargeable by the Commissioners of Customs and Excise on the supply to the Employer of any goods and/or services by the Contractor under the Contract.

Disputes (3)   If any dispute or question arises between either the Employer or the Contractor and the Commissioners of Customs and Excise in relation to any tax chargeable or alleged to be chargeable in connection with the Contract or the Works each shall render to the other such support and assistance as may be necessary to resolve the dispute or question.

Clause 66 not applicable (4)   Clause 66 shall not apply to any dispute or question arising under this Clause.

SPECIAL CONDITIONS

Special Conditions **71** The following Special Conditions form part of the Conditions of Contract.

(Note: Any Special Conditions including contract price fluctuation which it is desired to incorporate in the Conditions of Contract should be numbered consecutively with the foregoing Conditions of Contract).

SHORT DESCRIPTION OF WORKS

All the design and Permanent and Temporary Works in connection with* ....

....

....

Form of Tender

(NOTE: The Appendix forms part of the Tender)

To ....

....

....

GENTLEMEN,

Having examined the Employer's Requirements for the above-mentioned Works as set out in your communication of .... the Conditions of Contract (and the matters set out in the Appendix hereto) we offer to design construct and complete the said Works in conformity with the said Requirements and Conditions of Contract and with the other documents listed below for the sum of ....

....

.... (£ ....)

or such other sum as may be ascertained in accordance with the said Conditions of Contract.

If our tender is accepted we will if required provide security for the due performance of the Contract as stipulated in the Conditions of Contract and the Appendix hereto.

Unless and until a formal Agreement is prepared and executed this tender together with your written acceptance thereof shall form a binding Contract between us.

We understand that you are not bound to accept the lowest or any tender you may receive.

We are, Gentlemen,
Yours faithfully,

Signature ....

Address ....

....

Date ....

Other documents referred to above.
Appendix to Form of Tender Parts 1 and 2.

....

....

....

....

* Complete as appropriate.

FORM OF TENDER (APPENDIX)

(NOTE: Relevant Clause numbers are shown in brackets)

Appendix – Part 1 (to be completed prior to the invitation of Tenders)

1 Name of the Employer (Clause 1(1)(a)) ....

Address ....

2 Name of Employer's Representative (if known) (Clauses 1(1)(c) and 2(2)) ....

....

3 Defects Correction Period (Clause 1(1)(p)) .... weeks

4 Quality assurance (Clause 8(3)) Required/Not required

5 Contract Agreement (Clause 9) Required/Not required

6 Performance security (Clause 10(1)) Required/Not required

Amount (if required) to be .... % of estimated Contract Price

7 Minimum amount of third party insurance (Clause 23(3)) £ ....
each and every occurence

8 Commencement Date (if known) (Clause 41(1)(a)) ....

9 Time for completion (Clause 43) [a]

EITHER for the whole of the Works .... weeks

OR for Sections of the Works (Clause 1(1)(r))[b]

Section A .... weeks

Section B .... weeks

Section C .... weeks

the remainder of the Works .... weeks

10 Liquidated damages for delay (Clause 47)

	per day/week	limit of liabilility [c]
EITHER for the whole Works	£	£ ....
OR for Section A (as above)	£	£ ....
Section B (as above)	£	£ ....
Section C (as above)	£	£ ....
the remainder of the Works	£	£ ....

11 Vesting of materials not on Site (Clauses 54(2) & 60(1)(d)) (if required by the Employer)[d]

1 .... 4 ....

2 .... 5 ....

3 .... 6 ....

12 Percentage of the value of goods and materials to be included
in interim certificates (Clause 60(2)(ii))   .... %

13 Minimum amount of interim certificates (Clause 60(3))   £ ....

14 Rate of retention (Clause 60(5)(a)) (recommended not to exceed 5%)   .... %

15 Limit of retention (if any)   £ ....

16 Bank whose base lending rate is to be used (Clause 60(7)) ....

[a] If not stated, it is to be completed by the Contractor in Part 2 of the Appendix.

[b] To be completed, if required, with brief description. Where Sectional completion applies the item for "the Remainder of the Works" must be used to cover the balance of the Works if the Sections described do not in total comprise the whole of the Works.

[c] Delete where not required.

[d] (If used). Materials to which Clauses apply must be listed in Part 1 (Employer's option) or Part 2 (Contractor's option).

Appendix – Part 2

(To be completed by the tenderer)

1 Insurance policy excesses (Clause 25(2))

   Insurance of the Works (Clause 21(1))   £ ....

   Third party (property damage) (Clause 23(1))   £ ....

2 Time for completion of the Works (Clause 43) (if not completed in Part 1 of the Appendix)

   EITHER for the whole of the Works   .... weeks

   OR for sections of the Works (Clause 1(1)(r))

   Section A .... weeks

   Section B .... weeks

   Section C .... weeks

   the remainder of the Works   .... weeks

3 Vesting of materials not on Site (Clauses 54(2) & 60(1)(d)) (if required by the Contractor)

   1 ....   4 ....

   2 ....   5 ....

   3 ....   6 ....

4 Percentage adjustment for Prime Cost Items (Clause 58(2))   .... %

5 Contractor's designer (Clause 4(2)(a))

   The design work for which the Contractor is responsible will be carried out by

   ....

   ....

   ....

   ....

   ....

   Elements for which the Contractor has not yet appointed a designer.

   ....

   ....

   ....

Form of Agreement

THIS AGREEMENT made the .... day of .... 19 ....

BETWEEN ....

of ....

in the County of .... (hereinafter called "the Employer")

and ....

of ....

in the County of .... (hereinafter called "the Contractor").

WHEREAS the Employer is desirous that certain Works should be designed and constructed namely the Permanent and Temporary Works in connection with ....

....

....

and has reached agreement with the Contractor on the terms of a contract for the design construction and completion of such Works.

NOW THIS AGREEMENT WITNESSETH as follows

1. In this Agreement words and expressions shall have the same meanings as are respectively assigned to them in the Conditions of Contract hereinafter referred to.

2. The following documents shall be deemed to form and be read and construed as part of this Agreement namely

    (a) the Conditions of Contract

    (b) the Employer's Requirements

    (c) the Contractor's Submission and the written acceptance thereof

    (d) the following documents

....

....

....

....

....

....

....

3. In consideration of the payments to be made by the Employer to the Contractor as hereinafter mentioned the Contractor hereby convenants with the Employer to design construct and complete the works in conformity in all respects with the provisons of the Contract.

4. The Employer hereby convenants to pay to the Contractor in consideration of the design construction and completion of the Works the Contract Price at the times and in the manner prescribed by the Contract.

IN WITNESS whereof the parties hereto have caused this Agreement to be executed the day and year first above written.

SIGNED on behalf of the said .... Ltd/plc

Signature ....

Position ....

In the presence of ....

....

SIGNED on behalf of the said .... Ltd/plc

Signature ....

Position ....

In the presence of ....

....

or
SIGNED [and SEALED*] AS A DEED by the said ....

.... Ltd/plc

in the presence of ....

or
SIGNED [and SEALED*] AS A DEED by the said ....

.... Ltd/plc

in the presence of ....

*Delete as appropriate.

Form of Bond

BY THIS BOND

¹I ....

¹**Appropriate to an individual***

of ....

in the County of ....

²We .... Ltd/plc

²**Appropriate to a Limited Company***

whose registered office is at ....

in the County of ....

³We ....

³**Appropriate to a firm***

and ....

carrying on business in partnership under the name of style of ....

....

at ....

in the County of .... (hereinafter called "the Contractor")

⁴and .... Ltd/plc

⁴**Appropriate where the Surety is a Bank or Insurance Co.**

whose registered office is at ....

in the County of .... (hereinafter called "the Surety")

are held and firmly bound unto ....

(hereinafter called "the Employer") in the sum of

.... pounds

(£ ....) for the payment of which sum the Contractor and the Surety bind themselves their successors and assigns jointly and severally by these presents.

EXECUTED by the Contractor and the Surety this

.... day of .... 19 ....

***Delete as appropriate**

WHEREAS the Contractor and the Employer have entered into a Contract (hereinafter called "the said Contract") for the design construction and completion of the Works as therein mentioned in conformity with the provisions of the said Contract

NOW THE CONDITIONS of the above written Bond are such that if

(a) the Contractor (subject to Condition (c) hereof) duly performs and observes all the terms provisions conditions and stipulations of the said Contract on the Contractor's part to be performed and observed according to the true purport intent and meaning thereof or if

(b) on default by the Contractor the Surety satisfies and discharges the damages sustained by the Employer thereby up to the amount of the above written Bond or if

(c) the Employer's Representative defined in Clause 1(1)(c) of the said Contract issues a Defects Correction Certificate under Clause 61 of the said Contract then upon the date stated therein (herinafter called "the Relevant Date")

this obligation shall be null and void but otherwise shall remain in full force and effect.

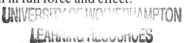

51

The Surety shall not in any way be released from any liability under the above written Bond by any

   (i)   alteration in the terms of the said Contract made by agreement between the Employer and the Contractor or

  (ii)   alteration in the extent or nature of the Works to be designed constructed and completed thereunder or

 (iii)   allowance of time by the Employer or the Employer's Representative under the said Contract or

 (iv)   forebearance or forgiveness in or in respect of any matter or thing concerning the said Contract on the part of the Employer or the Employer's Representative.

   PROVIDED ALWAYS that if any dispute arises between the Employer and the Contractor concerning the Relevant Date or the withholding of the Defects Correction Certificate then for the purposes of this Bond only and without prejudice to any resolution or determination pursuant to the provisions of the said Contract of any dispute whatever between the Employer and the Contractor the Relevant Date shall be

(A)   such date as may be agreed in writing between the Employer and the Contractor or

(B)   determined by arbitration as follows.

     (1)   The aggreived party shall forthwith by notice in writing to the other party refer the matter to the arbitration of a person to be agreed upon by the parties.

     (2)   If the parties fail to appoint an arbitrator within one calendar month of service of the said notice the dispute shall be referred to a person to be appointed on the application of either party by the President for the time being of the Institution of Civil Engineers.

     (3)   If an arbitrator declines the appointment or after appointment is removed by order of a competent court or is incapable of acting or dies and the parties do not within one calendar month of the vacancy arising fill the vacancy then either party may apply to the President for the time being of the Institution of Civil Engineers to appoint another arbitrator to fill the vacancy.

     (4)   In any case where the President for the time being of the Institution of Civil Engineers is not able to exercise the functions conferred on him and the said functions may be exercised on his behalf by a Vice-President for the time being of the said Institution.

     (5)   The arbitrator appointed in accordance with the foregoing provisions shall forthwith and with all due expedition enter upon the reference and make an award thereon. Such award shall be final and conclusive to determine the Relevant Date for the purposes of this Bond.

SIGNED [and SEALED*] AS A DEED by the said ....

.... Ltd/plc

in the presence of ....

SIGNED [and SEALED*] AS A DEED by the said ....

.... Ltd/plc

in the presence of ....

  * Delete as appropriate.